*This book is dedicated to Barbara G. Walker,
whose enormous contribution to knitting literature
has been inspiring and helping knitters like me
for many years.*

Contents

Introduction...8

1 Cable Basics...10
Terminology...12
Symbols for Charting...14
Working Cable Crossings...23

2 Simple Cables...44
Standard Rope Cables...46
Varying Cable Size...48
Changing the Proportions...50
Combinations...55
Double-Crossing Cables...62

3 Angles and Curves...64
Angles...66
Diamonds...76
Curves and Circles...90

4 Braids and Pretzels...98
Braids...100
Pretzels...110
Combining Braids and Pretzels...120

Cable Left
Cable Right

94 Knitted Cables

JUDITH DURANT

PHOTOGRAPHY BY
MARS VILAUBI

Storey Publishing

The mission of Storey Publishing is to serve our customers by publishing practical information that encourages personal independence in harmony with the environment.

Edited by Gwen Steege
Art direction and book design by Mary Winkelman Velgos
Text production by Jennifer Jepson Smith
Technical edit by Kate Atherley
Indexed by Nancy D. Wood

Cover photography by John Polak (front) and Mars Vilaubi (back)
Interior photography by Mars Vilaubi
Charts by the author

Storey Publishing
210 MASS MoCA Way
North Adams, MA 01247
www.storey.com

Printed in China by R.R. Donnelley
10 9 8 7 6 5 4 3 2 1

LIBRARY OF CONGRESS CATALOGING-IN-PUBLICATION DATA

Names: Durant, Judith, 1955– author.
Title: Cable left, cable right : 94 knitted cables / Judith Durant.
Description: North Adams, MA : Storey Publishing, 2016. | Includes index.
Identifiers: LCCN 2015044820 | ISBN 9781612125169 (pbk. : alk. paper) | ISBN 9781612125176 (ebook)
Subjects: LCSH: Cable knitting. | Knitting—Technique.
Classification: LCC TT820 .D843 2016 | DDC 746.43/2—dc23
LC record available at http://lccn.loc.gov/2015044820

5 Fillers, Ribbings, and Allover Patterns...126

Fillers...128

Ribbings...136

Allover Patterns...142

6 Dressing Up Your Cables...154

Adding Texture and Bobbles...156

Two-Color Cables...170

Beading Up Your Cables...180

Reversible Cable Methods...190

7 Design Considerations...198

Balancing Patterns Vertically...200

Balancing Patterns Horizontally...201

Coping with Take-Up and Splay...204

Decreasing and Increasing in Cable
Patterns...208

Index...214

Acknowledgments...216

Introduction
The World of Cables

Welcome to the world of knitted cables, where a simple alteration to a basic pattern can become a new and unique design. My goal here is to explain the fundamentals of cable technique so you can not only look at a fisherman knit sweater and know how it was done, you can even design your own.

Cables twist to the right or to the left, depending on how you manipulate the stitches. Cables can twist together like ropes or travel apart and come together again, crossing or not. They can stand alone in a panel, or they can be repeated to create an allover design. Cables can float on a ground of reverse stockinette stitch, or they can be filled in with moss or seed stitch. They can be worked for the entire length of a fabric, or they can stand alone and look like appliqués. They can even form ribbing and be used to pull in the bottom of a hat or a sweater.

In this book we'll explore rope cables and other basic cables; angles and curves, including diamonds and circles; pretzels and braids; and fillers, ribbings, and allover patterns. Then we can spice things up by adding texture, color, and even beads to the cables. We'll even dip into the world of creating reversible cables. The basic math necessary to combine cables of varied width and length will be covered, as will how to compensate for cable take-up and splay.

You'll also learn how to read cable charts. Various publications use different symbols to mean the same thing, but the methods of creating the cables remain the same. With charted designs you can see from the symbol how many stitches are involved in turning the cable, whether the cable will be crossing right or left, whether it uses only knit stitches or a combination of knit and

purl, and any other details specific to the particular crossing.

Plain or fancy, cables allow you to make a one-of-a-kind product. You can choose from among the hundreds of cable designs that are available in books such as *A Treasury of Knitting Patterns*, *A Second Treasury of Knitting Patterns*, or *Charted Knitting Designs*, all by Barbara Walker; Vogue Knitting *Stitchionary 2: Cables*; The Harmony Guides *220 Aran Stitches and Patterns*; or other collections. And with the understanding you gain here, you can alter any of those cable designs to make them unique, or even create your own.

Knit and cable on,

Judith Durant

CHAPTER 1

Cable
Basics

What is a knitted cable? The basis of a cable is that 1 or more stitches crosses 1 or more stitches immediately to the left or right of the original stitches; then all the stitches are knitted in this new order to create a pattern. To make the switch, a designated number of stitches is slipped to a cable needle; the cable needle is then held in front or in back of the work while you work a designated number of stitches from the left needle; finally, you work the stitches on the cable needle. The result will be a design of stitches that cross to the left or to the right, depending on whether you hold the cable needle with stitches in front or in back.

TERMINOLOGY

Throughout the knitting literature available today, there are several terms used for the same cable action. For example, let's look at a 4-stitch cable where 2 stitches change places with the adjacent 2 stitches.

If the crossing goes to the left, you may see this cable called any of the following:

C4L, cable four left

C4F, cable four front

4LC, four left cross

4FC, four front cross

2/2LC, two over two left cross

2/2FC, two over two front cross

2/2L, two over two left

2/2F, two over two front

If the crossing goes to the right, you'd see R (right) where the L appears or B (back) where the F appears in these names.

Now throw into the mix that cables can be worked in a combination of knit and purl stitches, meaning that knit stitches cross over purl stitches, and you may see these descriptors:

C4LP, cable four left purl

C4FP, cable four front purl

4LCP, four left cross purl

4FCP, four front cross purl

2/2LCP, two over two left cross purl

2/2FCP, two over two front cross purl

2/2LP, two over two left purl

2/2FP, two over two front purl

Since it is possible to make a cable crossing with 4 stitches that has 3 stitches crossing over 1, or vice versa, you can see that it can become quite confusing. For this reason, I use the 2/2 naming convention; if the crossing has 3 stitches over 1, it becomes 3/1. I also prefer the L for left and R for right rather than F for front and B for back — the top stitches move left or right, and I can be sure I've got it right by looking at it.

Because there is no standard, be sure you carefully read the explanations for cables in whatever publication you're using.

SYMBOLS FOR CHARTING

The best way to present cable instructions is with charts. A chart can visually describe what is happening by showing a left or right cross, as well as knit and purl stitches.

In the next few pages, you'll find symbols for the cable crossings used in this book. The key shows the symbol used, the abbreviation, and the method. Beginning on page 20, you'll find a key to the other non-cable symbols used in the charts presented here.

Cable Symbols

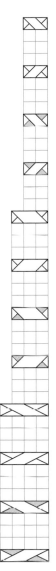

1/1L. Slip 1 stitch to cable needle and hold in front, knit 1 from left needle, knit 1 from cable needle.

1/1R. Slip 1 stitch to cable needle and hold in back, knit 1 from left needle, knit 1 from cable needle.

1/1LP. Slip 1 stitch to cable needle and hold in front, purl 1 from left needle, knit 1 from cable needle.

1/1RP. Slip 1 stitch to cable needle and hold in back, knit 1 from left needle, purl 1 from cable needle.

2/1L. Slip 2 stitches to cable needle and hold in front, knit 1 from left needle, knit 2 from cable needle.

2/1R. Slip 1 stitch to cable needle and hold in back, knit 2 from left needle, knit 1 from cable needle.

2/1LP. Slip 2 stitches to cable needle and hold in front, purl 1 from left needle, knit 2 from cable needle.

2/1RP. Slip 1 stitch to cable needle and hold in back, knit 2 from left needle, purl 1 from cable needle.

2/2L. Slip 2 stitches to cable needle and hold in front, knit 2 from left needle, knit 2 from cable needle.

2/2R. Slip 2 stitches to cable needle and hold in back, knit 2 from left needle, knit 2 from cable needle.

2/2LP. Slip 2 stitches to cable needle and hold in front, purl 2 from left needle, knit 2 from cable needle.

2/2RP. Slip 2 stitches to cable needle and hold in back, knit 2 from left needle, purl 2 from cable needle.

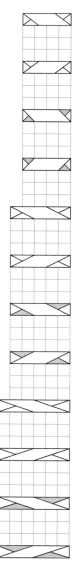

3/1L. Slip 3 stitches to cable needle and hold in front, knit 1 from left needle, knit 3 from cable needle.

3/1R. Slip 1 stitch to cable needle and hold in back, knit 3 from left needle, knit 1 from cable needle.

3/1LP. Slip 3 stitches to cable needle and hold in front, purl 1 from left needle, knit 3 from cable needle.

3/1RP. Slip 1 stitch to cable needle and hold in back, knit 3 from left needle, purl 1 from cable needle.

3/2L. Slip 3 stitches to cable needle and hold in front, knit 2 from left needle, knit 3 from cable needle.

3/2R. Slip 2 stitches to cable needle and hold in back, knit 3 from left needle, knit 2 from cable needle.

3/2LP. Slip 3 stitches to cable needle and hold in front, purl 2 from left needle, knit 3 from cable needle.

3/2RP. Slip 2 stitches to cable needle and hold in back, knit 3 from left needle, purl 2 from cable needle.

3/3L. Slip 3 stitches to cable needle and hold in front, knit 3 from left needle, knit 3 from cable needle.

3/3R. Slip 3 stitches to cable needle and hold in back, knit 3 from left needle, knit 3 from cable needle.

3/3LP. Slip 3 stitches to cable needle and hold in front, purl 3 from left needle, knit 3 from cable needle.

3/3RP. Slip 3 stitches to cable needle and hold in back, knit 3 from left needle, purl 3 from cable needle.

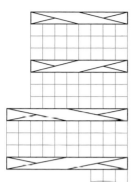

4/4L. Slip 4 stitches to cable needle and hold in front, knit 4 from left needle, knit 4 from cable needle.

4/4R. Slip 4 stitches to cable needle and hold in back, knit 4 from left needle, knit 4 from cable needle.

5/5L. Slip 5 stitches to cable needle and hold in front, knit 5 from left needle, knit 5 from cable needle.

5/5R. Slip 5 stitches to cable needle and hold in back, knit 5 from left needle, knit 5 from cable needle.

1/2L. Slip 1 stitch to cable needle and hold in front, knit 2 from left needle, knit 1 from cable needle.

1/2R. Slip 2 stitches to cable needle and hold in back, knit 1 from left needle, knit 2 from cable needle.

1/2/1L. Slip 1 stitch to cable needle 1 and hold in front, slip 2 stitches to cable needle 2 and hold in back; knit 1 from left needle, knit 2 from cable needle 2, knit 1 from cable needle 1.

1/2/1R. Slip 3 stitches to cable needle and hold in back, knit 1 from left needle, slip 2 leftmost stitches from cable needle to left needle, move cable needle to front, knit 2 from left needle, knit 1 from cable needle.

2/1/2LP. Slip 2 stitches to cable needle 1 and hold in front, slip 1 stitch to cable needle 2 and hold in back; knit 2 from left needle, slip 1 from cable needle 2 to left needle and purl it, knit 2 from cable needle 1.

2/1/2RP. Slip 3 stitches to cable needle and hold in back, knit 2 from left needle, leftmost stitch from cable needle to left needle and purl it, knit 2 from cable needle.

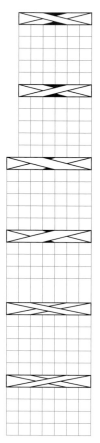

2/2/2LP. Slip 2 stitches to cable needle 1 and hold in front, slip 2 stitches to cable needle 2 and hold in back; knit 2 from left needle, purl 2 from cable needle 2, knit 2 from cable needle 1.

2/2/2RP. Slip 4 stitches to cable needle and hold in back, knit 2 from left needle, slip 2 from cable needle to left needle, hold cable needle in front and purl 2 from left needle, knit 2 from cable needle.

3/1/3LP. Slip 3 stitches to cable needle 1 and hold in front, slip 1 stitch to cable needle 2 and hold in back; knit 3 from left needle, purl 1 from cable needle 2, knit 3 from cable needle 1.

3/1/3RP. Slip 4 stitches to cable needle and hold in back, knit 3 from left needle, slip leftmost stitch from cable needle to left needle, hold cable needle in front, and purl 1 from left needle, knit 3 from cable needle.

2/3/2L. Slip 2 stitches to cable needle 1 and hold in front, slip 3 stitches to cable needle 2 and hold in back; knit 2 from left needle, knit 3 from cable needle 2, knit 2 from cable needle 1.

2/3/2R. Slip 5 stitches to cable needle and hold in back, knit 2 from left needle, slip 3 from cable needle to left needle, hold cable needle in front and knit 3 from left needle, knit 2 from cable needle.

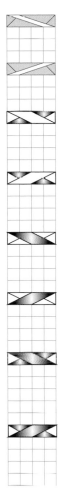

1/3LP. Slip 1 stitch to cable needle and hold in front, purl 3 from left needle, knit 1 from cable needle.

1/3RP. Slip 3 stitches to cable needle and hold in back, knit 1 from left needle, purl 3 from cable needle.

2/2L Decorative. Slip 2 stitches to cable needle and hold in front, work 2 from left needle according to instructions, knit 2 from cable needle.*

2/2R Decorative. Slip 2 stitches to cable needle and hold in back, knit 2 from left needle, work 2 from cable needle according to instructions.*

2/2L Bold Decorative. Slip 2 stitches to cable needle and hold in front, knit 2 from left needle, work 2 from cable needle according to instructions.*

2/2R Bold Decorative. Slip 2 stitches to cable needle and hold in back, work 2 from left needle according to instructions, knit 2 from cable needle.*

2/2L Double Bold. Slip 2 stitches to cable needle and hold in front, work 2 from left needle according to instructions, work 2 from cable needle according to instructions.*

2/2R Double Bold. Slip 2 stitches to cable needle and hold in back, work 2 from left needle according to instructions, work 2 from cable needle according to instructions.*

* These instructions apply to decorative cables of all sizes. Work a decorative cable as for a regular cable, adding the decorative stitch, color, or bead to the part of the cable indicated by the gradient coloring.

Other Symbols

☐   Knit on right side, purl on wrong side.

•   Purl on right side, knit on wrong side.

○   Yarnover.

Ω   Knit through back on right side, purl through back on wrong side.

▨   No stitch — ignore this block of chart.

▪   Work stitch in contrasting color.

╱   Knit 2 stitches together (k2tog).

╲   Slip 1 knitwise, slip another knitwise, place left needle into front of 2 slipped stitches and knit them together through the back loop (ssk).

⅄   Slip 1, knit 2 together, pass the slipped stitch over the k2tog (sk2p).

╱   Knit 3 together (k3tog).

Y   Insert left needle from back to front under strand between the needles; knit the stitch through the front.

X   Insert left needle from front to back under strand between the needles; knit the stitch through the back.

Ⓥ   Knit 1 but do not drop from needle, yarn over, knit 1 into same stitch — 1 stitch increased to 3.

V   Knit 1 through the back but do not drop from needle, knit 1 into same stitch; insert left needle behind vertical strand between the 2 stitches just made and knit the strand through the back loop — 1 stitch increased to 3.

Ⓥ₃   Knit in front, back, and front of same stitch — 1 stitch increased to 3.

■   Pattern repeat.

Slip 4 stitches to right needle, *pass second stitch over first (center) stitch and off needle; slip center stitch to left needle, slip second stitch over center stitch and off needle; slip center stitch to right needle; repeat from * two more times, end leaving center stitch on left needle; knit the center stitch — 7 stitches decreased to 1.

Work as for 7-to-1 decrease above but slip 3 stitches to right needle and repeat from * one more time — 5 stitches decreased to 1.

B Make bobble of choice in 1 stitch (see page 158).

B Make bobble of choice in 2 stitches (see page 158).

Bind 2. Yo, p2, pass yo over purl stitches.

Bind 3. Slip 1 with yarn in back. knit 1, yo, knit 1, pass slipped stitch over the k1, yo, k1.

Wrap 4. Slip 4 stitches to cable needle, wrap yarn around the 4 stitches twice; with yarn in back, knit 4 from cable needle.

Bead knitting. With beads prestrung, knit a bead into the stitch on right side, purl a bead into the stitch on wrong side (see page 188).

Hook bead knitting. With small crochet hook, pick up a bead, remove stitch from left needle with the hook, slide bead down onto stitch; return stitch to left needle and knit it (see page 180).

Slip stitch bead knitting. With beads prestrung on yarn, bring yarn forward, slip 2 stitches to right needle, slide up 2 beads, bring needle to back leaving 2 beads in front of 2 slipped stitches and continue in pattern (see page 188).

Cable Needle Varieties

There are a few options when it comes to cable needles. One is not better than another — you just need to find the one that's most comfortable for you. Note that for some cables you'll need two cable needles, so be sure you have more than one available.

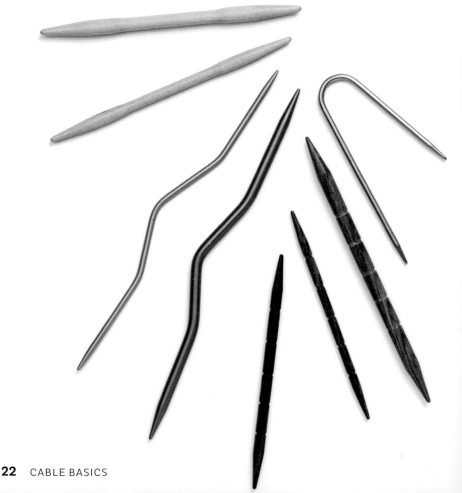

WORKING CABLE CROSSINGS

Let's get to the knitting! Here we'll look at how to make left-crossing cables, right-crossing cables, cables with knit and purl stitches, and cables that cross in two directions over a stationary stitch or stitches. In the examples that follow, I show a specific number of stitches being crossed, but the same principles apply to crossing with various stitch counts. Unless otherwise specified, slip all stitches onto the cable needle purlwise.

Left-Crossing Cables

To work a left-crossing cable, you'll hold the stitches on the cable needle in front of the work while you work the following stitches from the left needle. I remember that left is held in front because both words contain the letter "f."

3 over 3 Left (3/3L)

1 Slip 3 stitches from left needle onto cable needle.

2 Hold cable needle with stitches in front of work.

 Knit 3 stitches from left
needle.

④ Knit 3 stitches from cable
needle.

Completed.

Right-Crossing Cables

To work a right-crossing cable, you'll hold the stitches on the cable needle in back of the work while you work the following stitches from the left needle. In my mind I change "back" to "rear" so I can remember that right is held in the rear because they both begin with the letter "r."

3 over 3 Right (3/3R)

1 Slip 3 stitches from left needle onto cable needle.

2 Hold cable needle with stitches in back of work.

3 Knit 3 stitches from left needle.

④ Knit 3 stitches from cable needle.

Completed.

Knit-over-Purl Cable Crossings

Crossing knit stitches over purls is used to form lattice patterns, diamonds, closed rings, and other cables. The same principles of holding stitches to the front to cross left and to the back to cross right apply.

3 over 1 Left Purl (3/1LP)

① Slip 3 knit stitches from left needle onto cable needle.

2 Hold cable needle with stitches in front of work.

3 Purl 1 stitch from left needle.

4 Knit 3 stitches from cable needle.

Completed.

3 over 1 Right Purl (3/1RP)

1 Slip 1 purl stitch from left needle onto cable needle.

2 Hold cable needle with stitch in back of work.

3 Knit 3 stitches from left needle.

4 Purl 1 stitch from cable needle.

Completed.

Double-Crossing Cables

Double-crossing cables consist of 1 or more outer stitches crossing over a stable center stitch or stitches. This involves both left and right crossings, and some require two cable needles. These examples are worked over 4 stitches. In the first example the fourth stitch crosses the other 3 from left to right; then the first stitch crosses the 2 center stitches from right to left. In the second example the fourth stitch crosses the 2 center stitches from left to right; then the first stitch crosses the other 3 from right to left.

1/2/1 Right (1/2/1R)

1 Slip 3 stitches to cable needle.

2 Hold cable needle with stitches in back of work.

3 Knit 1 stitch from left needle.

4 Slip the leftmost 2 stitches from cable needle to left needle.

5 Hold cable needle with 1 stitch in front of work.

6 Knit 2 stitches from left needle.

7 Knit 1 stitch from cable needle.

Completed.

1/2/1 Left (1/2/1L)

1 Slip 1 stitch to cable needle 1 and 2 stitches to cable needle 2.

2 Hold cable needle 1 with stitch in front of work; hold cable needle 2 with stitches in back of work.

3 Knit 1 stitch from left needle.

4 Knit 2 stitches from cable needle 2.

5 Knit 1 stitch from cable needle 1.

Completed.

Knitting Cables without a Cable Needle

Many knitters like to work cables without a cable needle, claiming that it's easier and faster. I have not generally found this to be the case, as I end up having to reconstruct stitches that come undone in the process. However, I often work without a needle when working a 1/1 crossing because it's not necessary to drop unworked stitches from the needle. The idea with more than 2 stitches is that you reorder the stitches onto the left needle in the finished cable order before knitting, and then knit them in the "new" order. The technique works for many, so I present the option here.

1 over 1 Left (1/1L)

1 Pass right needle behind first stitch on left needle, and insert it into the second stitch through front loop. *Note:* You may also work this stitch through the back loop if you find this easier — there is almost no difference in the finished look.

2 Knit the stitch, and leave it on the needle.

③ Insert the right needle into the first stitch on left needle.

④ Knit the stitch, and drop both from the left needle.

1 over 1 Right (1/1R)

① Pass right needle in front of first stitch on left needle, and insert it into the front loop of the second stitch.

② Knit the stitch, and leave it on the left needle.

③ Insert the right needle into the first stitch on left needle.

④ Knit the stitch, and drop both from the left needle.

2 over 2 Left (2/2L)

① Drop 4 stitches from left needle, and hold them between the right index finger and thumb.

② Pass the left needle in front of stitches 4 and 3, and slip stitches 2 and 1 onto left needle, continuing to hold stitches 4 and 3 firmly.

3 Pick up stitches 4 and 3 onto right needle.

4 Slip stitches 4 and 3 from right to left needle.

5 Knit 4.

Note: It's the same idea for cables of other numbers of stitches. Remove all the stitches in the cable from the left needle, leave the prescribed number of stitches in midair while you slip the others onto the left needle, then slip the remaining stitches onto the left needle, and work all stitches.

2 over 2 Right (2/2R)

1 Drop 4 stitches from left needle, and hold them between the right index finger and thumb.

2 Pass the left needle in back of stitches 4 and 3, and slip stitches 2 and 1 onto left needle, continuing to hold stitches 4 and 3 firmly.

3 Pick up stitches 4 and 3 onto right needle.

4 Slip stitches 4 and 3 from right to left needle.

⑤ Knit 4.

Completed.

2 over 2 Left (2/2L) Alternate

1 Insert the right needle into the third and fourth stitches on the left needle from behind.

2 Slip the stitches to the right needle, dropping the first and second stitches.

3 Pick up stitches 2 then 1 with the left needle.

4 Slip the fourth and third stitches back onto the left needle.

5 Knit all 4 stitches.

2 over 2 Right (2/2R) Alternate

1 Insert the right needle into the third and fourth stitches on the left needle from the front.

2 Slip the stitches to the right needle, dropping the first and second stitches.

3 Pick up stitches 2 then 1 with the left needle.

4 Slip the fourth and third stitches back onto the left needle.

5 Knit all 4 stitches.

Tips for Cable Success

The most important part of knitting neat and even cables is to keep even tension as you work. That said, here are a few tips.

Loose Purl Stitches after a Cable

Because of the stress put on the stitches that compose a cable — pulling one set of stitches across another — the first purl stitch following a cable crossing may become loose. To compensate for this, try tugging a bit more on the working yarn while working the first 2 stitches after a cable.

Loose Knit Stitch at Cable Edge

Sometimes the last knit stitch of a cable, the one at the left edge, is looser than the others (A). This phenomenon also occurs when knitting ribbings and other knit/purl patterns. For some reason, transitioning from purl stitches to knit stitches works fine, but when moving from knit stitches to purl stitches, the last knit stitch often appears looser, or larger, than the others. One thing that can help this is to work the first purl stitch through the back

A

Another way to tighten that last knit stitch is to work the following purl stitch by wrapping the yarn clockwise, rather than the usual counter-clockwise, around the needle (C). This puts a twisted stitch on the needle. When you come to that stitch on the wrong-side row, knit it through the back loop to untwist it. However, I don't use this technique because, while it does definitely tighten that last knit stitch, it distorts the reverse stockinette stitch formed by the purl stitches.

loop, twisting it (B). When you come to the twisted stitch on the wrong-side row, knit it as usual, not through the back loop. This will help to tighten the last knit stitch of the cable and also take care of a loose purl stitch as mentioned on the facing page. The result is a twisted purl stitch, but this is hardly noticeable on the right side because the purl stitch is partially obscured by the last knit stitch of the cable.

Counting Rows

When working cable repeats of different lengths — for example, working a design with cable patterns that have 32-, 16-, 8-, and 2-row repeats — it's not easy to keep track of where you are in the various patterns in your head. If you're working with a chart that shows the entire pattern repeat, that is, the chart has 32 rows, it's easy: Simply make a photocopy of the chart and check off each row as you complete it. But patterns are

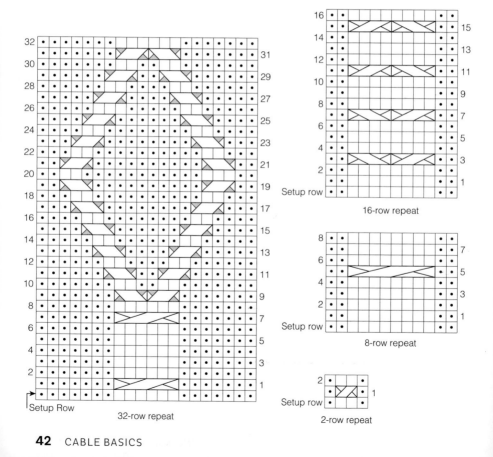

32-row repeat

16-row repeat

8-row repeat

2-row repeat

often presented with each cable pattern having its own chart. In this case make a 32-row grid that has a column for each cable. For this example, a 32-row pattern is in the center, then moving both to the right and the left there are 2-row, 8 row, 2-row, 16-row, 2-row, 8-row, and 2-row repeats. Assuming that the design begins with a half repeat, your grid might look like the one shown here. The numbers in the grid represent the last row of each cable pattern repeat. As you complete a row, check it off at the right of the grid.

Row																✓	
32	2		2		2		2		2		2		2		2		
																	31
30	2		2		2		2		2		2		2		2		
																	29
28	2	8	2		2	8	2		2	8	2		2	8	2		
																	27
26	2		2		2		2		2		2		2		2		
																	25
24	2		2	16	2		2		2		2	16	2		2		
																	23
22	2		2		2		2		2		2		2		2		
																	21
20	2	8	2		2	8	2		2	8	2		2	8	2		
																	19
18	2		2		2		2		2		2		2		2		
																	17
16	2		2		2		2	32	2		2		2		2		
																	15
14	2		2		2		2		2		2		2		2		
																	13
12	2	8	2		2	8	2		2	8	2		2	8	2		
																	11
10	2		2		2		2		2		2		2		2		
																	9
8	2		2	16	2		2		2		2	16	2		2		
																	7
6	2		2		2		2		2		2		2		2	✓	
																✓	5
4	2	8	2		2	8	2		2	8	2		2	8	2	✓	
																✓	3
2	2		2		2		2		2		2		2		2	✓	
																✓	1
Setup row																✓	

CHAPTER 2

Simple Cables

First we'll look at the simplest of cables, the ones that look like ropes. These have an even number of stitches. Divide these stitches in half, twist one half over the other, and you've got a cable. We'll vary the proportions, then combine methods to produce some interesting results. See chapter 1 for knitting techniques.

STANDARD ROPE CABLES

Rope cables can cross to the left or to the right. They are made in exactly the same way, except where you hold the stitches on the cable needle. You'll note that some of the patterns begin with a setup row worked on the wrong side. This is an option I sometimes employ, usually when transitioning from a ribbing.

3 over 3 Left (3/3L)

Left-Crossing Cable

Here is a 6-stitch cable that crosses to the left, meaning that 3 stitches move from right to left over 3 other stitches. As outlined in chapter 1, this means that the 3 stitches placed on the cable needle are held in front. This cable, 3 over 3 Left, is abbreviated 3/3L.

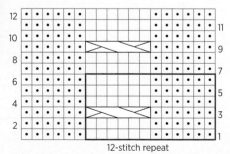

12-stitch repeat

Right-Crossing Cable

Here is a 6-stitch cable that crosses to the right, meaning that 3 stitches move from left to right over 3 other stitches. As outlined in chapter 1, this means that the 3 stitches placed on the cable needle are held in back. This cable, 3 over 3 Right, is abbreviated 3/3R.

3 over 3 Right (3/3R)

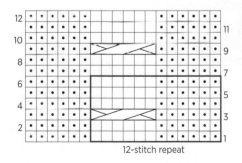

12-stitch repeat

VARYING CABLE SIZE

A good rule of thumb for rope cables is that the number of rows between crossings is equal to the number of stitches in the cable. In the two examples on pages 46–47, the 6-stitch cables are crossed every 6 rows. Here are a few other sizes.

Smaller Cables

A 4-stitch right-crossing cable (2/2R) is beside a 4-stitch left-crossing cable (2/2L), and the cables are crossed every 4 rows.

2/2L on Left, with 2/2R on Right

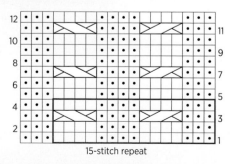

15-stitch repeat

Larger and Even Smaller Cables

Here an 8-stitch right-crossing cable (4/4R) is flanked by 2-stitch right- (1/1R) and left-crossing (1/1L) cables. For the 4/4R, place 4 stitches on a cable needle and hold in back, k4 from left needle, k4 from cable needle. For the 1/1R cables, hold 1 stitch in back, k1 from left needle, k1 from cable needle. For the 1/1L cables, hold 1 stitch in front, k1 from left needle, k1 from cable needle. Note that the 8-stitch cable crosses every 8 rows and the 2-stitch cable crosses every 2 rows. This swatch begins with a setup row, worked on the wrong side, making the 2-stitch cable ready for turning on the first right-side row.

4/4R Flanked by 1/1R on Right and 1/1L on Left

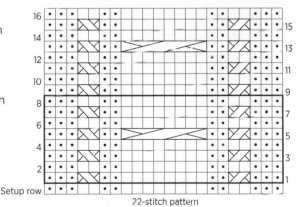

Setup row

22-stitch pattern

CHANGING THE PROPORTIONS

The standard proportions, as illustrated in the first four samples, use the rule of having the same number of rows in the repeat as there are stitches in the cable. Of course, rules are made to be broken, so here we'll do just that.

Elongated Cables

This is what it looks like to double the number of rows in the repeat — a 3/3R cable is turned every 12 rows. I like to work long cables with a half cable at the beginning and the end, as shown here (the first cable is turned after 4 plain rows and the last cable is followed by 5 plain rows). Work the chart for the desired number of cables, ending the last repeat with Row 10.

3/3R Elongated

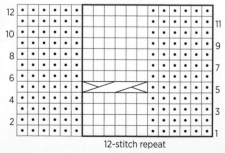

12-stitch repeat

Super-Elongated Cables

Here's a 3/3R cable that crosses every 24 rows. Again, it begins and ends with a half cable (the first cable is turned after 10 plain rows and the last cable is followed by 11 plain rows). Work the chart for the desired number of cables, ending the last chart repeat on Row 22.

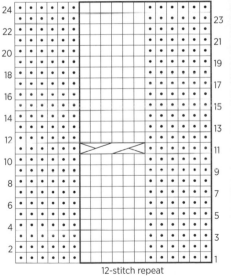

12-stitch repeat

3/3R Super-Elongated

Condensed Cables

This 3/3R cable is turned every 4 rows. The cabled area is a bit thick and stiff, so consider the type of project before working a lot of these cables. This would work well for handbags.

3/3R Condensed

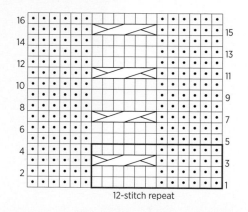

12-stitch repeat

Varying the Crossings

You can make things more interesting by crossing the cables after different numbers of rows. This sample shows a 3/3R 12-row cable, followed by a 3/3R 4-row cable, and finished with another 12 rows. Work the chart for the desired number of repeats, then work Rows 1–10 once more.

3/3R with Varied Lengths

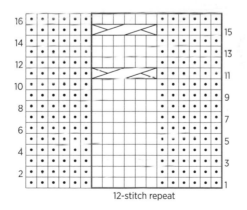

12-stitch repeat

Chunky Cables

You can't make a cable with fewer than 2 stitches, but you can use as many stitches as you want. Here's a 6/6R cable that crosses every 12 rows; you could also use 24 stitches and 24 rows. Or more. For this cable, work the chart for the desired number of repeats, ending the last repeat on Row 10.

6/6R

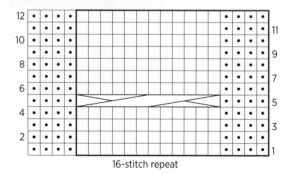

16-stitch repeat

COMBINATIONS

You can combine elements of the simple right- and left-crossing rope cables presented above to create even more interesting cable designs.

Separated Outward Double Cables

Two 4-stitch cables are side by side, separated by 1 purl stitch. The cable on the right is 2/2R, and the cable on the left is 2/2L.

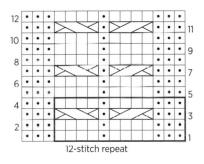

12-stitch repeat

2/2R on Right, with 2/2L on Left

Separated Inward Double Cables

This swatch is worked the same as the previous double cable, but the cable on the right is a 2/2L and the cable on the left is a 2/2R. Notice that this looks like the outward double cables on page 55 turned upside down. This comes in handy if you knit a sweater from the bottom up, then pick up stitches at the armholes and knit the sleeves from the top down — if you used outward cables on the body, you can use inward cables on the sleeves, and the patterns will match.

2/2L on Right, with 2/2R on Left

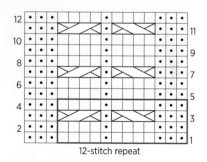

12-stitch repeat

United Outward Double Cables

A 3/3R and a 3/3L cable are worked here with no separating stitch between them. The result is a series of cables that looks something like wishbones.

3/3R on Right, with 3/3L on Left

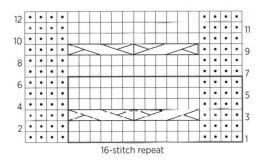

16-stitch repeat

United Inward Double Cables

Worked like the outward double cables on page 57 but in reverse order, the wishbones now appear to be upside down.

3/3L on Right, 3/3R on Left

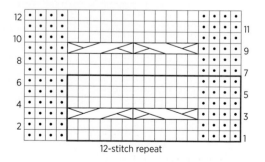

12-stitch repeat

Snaking Cable

This cable turns right, left, right, and left again by working 3/3R, 3/3L, 3/3R, and 3/3L. The result is a snaking cable that seems to float over the background.

3/3R, 3/3L, 3/3R, 3/3L

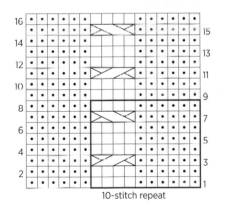

10-stitch repeat

Hourglass Cable

The hourglass effect is accomplished by uniting two Snaking Cables (page 59). The column on the right uses 3/3R followed by 3/3L, and the column on the left uses 3/3L followed by 3/3R. As with the Snaking Cable, this one seems to float over the background.

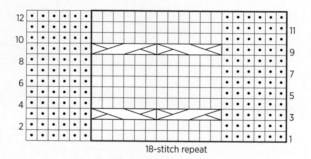

18-stitch repeat

3/3R followed by 3/3L, 3/3L
followed by 3/3R

DOUBLE-CROSSING CABLES

Double-crossing cables involve 1 or more stitches from the right side of the cable crossing left over 1 or more center stitches and 1 or more stitches from the left side of the cable crossing over the same center stitches. See page 29 in chapter 1 for instructions on working these cables.

4-Stitch Double-Crossing Cable

A 1/2/1R cable has 1 stitch from the right and 1 stitch from the left crossing over 2 center knit stitches.

1/2/1R Cable

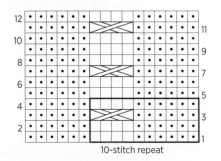

10-stitch repeat

7-Stitch Double-Crossing Cable

Here a 2/3/2R cable is worked with 2 stitches from the right and 2 stitches from the left crossing over 3 center stitches.

2/3/2R Cable

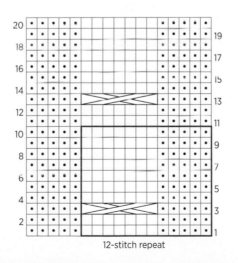

12-stitch repeat

CHAPTER 3

Angles and Curves

In this chapter we'll look at cabling that forms straight and curved lines. For these cables the crossings usually (I'd never say *always* with knitting) are made on every right-side row. And usually (same caveat) you'll cross 2 or more knit stitches to the right or the left over 1 purl stitch. For our purposes, using 2 or more knit stitches makes a cable — crossing with single stitches creates traveling stitch patterns. Depending on where and when you make the crossings, you'll get straight or curved lines.

ANGLES

Straight lines can be used to create diagonal patterns, zigzag patterns, X-crosses, and diamonds. In all but one of the following samples, the "cable" stitch or stitches move over 1 background stitch. We'll use both right and left crossings.

Simple Zigzag

This pattern uses repeating 3/1LP crossings followed by 3/1RP crossings to form a simple zigzag. At the point where we change from left to right crossings, 2 extra plain rows are worked to create a gentler zig. Or is that zag?

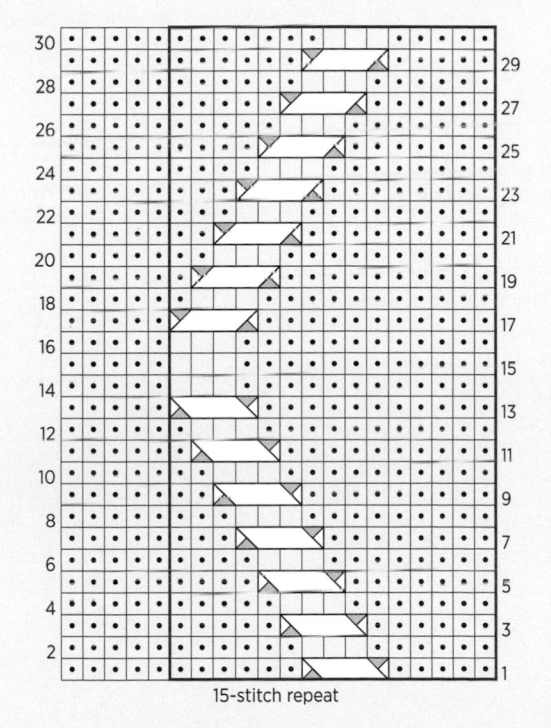

15-stitch repeat

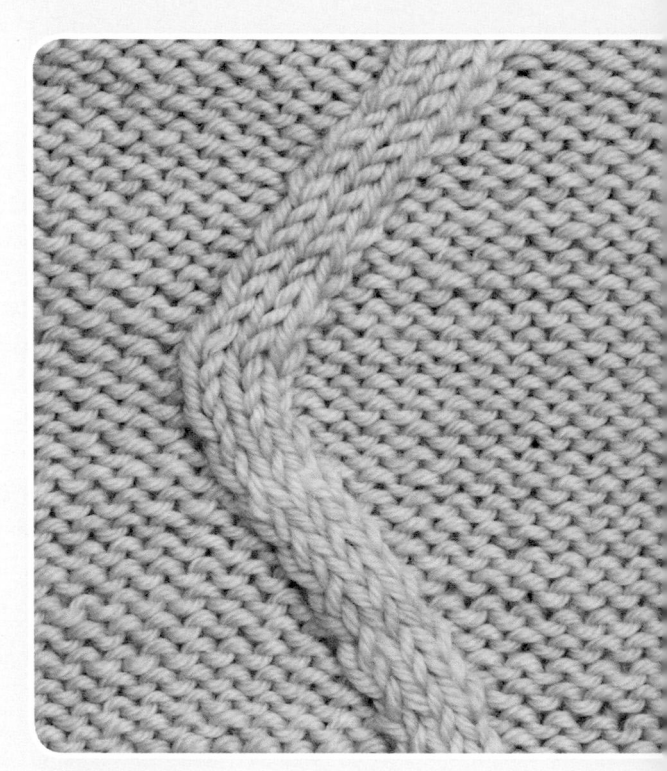

Simple Zigzag

X-Crossings

The group of four cables on the next few pages uses a combination of left and right crossings to create X patterns. You can vary the width of the design by adding more rows that have progressively more purl stitches between the crossings as you'll see on page 72. You can also interlock the X patterns by adding the same pattern to each side of the original X. This will produce an allover lattice pattern like those shown on pages 142 through 145.

The 3-Stitch X

At the bottom half of the design use 3/1LP crossings at the beginning and 3/1RP crossings at the end of the pattern rows, and at the top half of the design use 3/1RP crossings at the beginning and 3/1LP crossings at the end of the pattern rows to create a large X. When the two lines meet, you can use either a 3/3R or a 3/3L cross. This sample uses 3/3L.

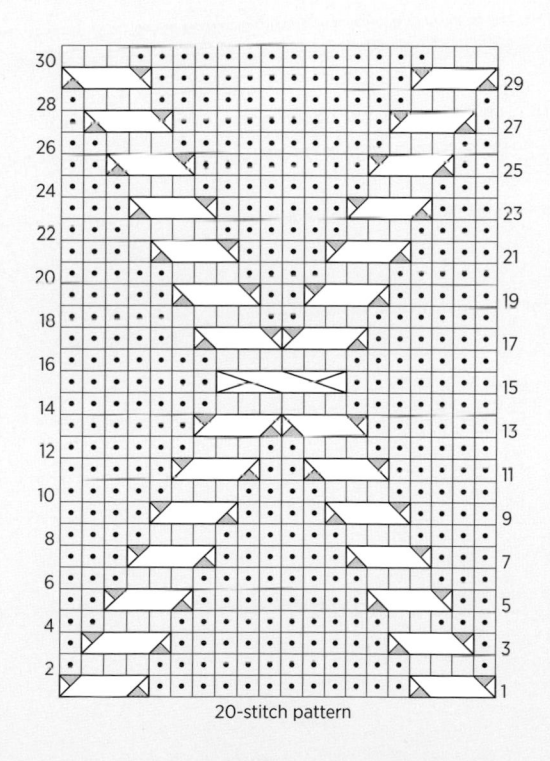

20-stitch pattern

The 3-Stitch X

The 2-Stitch X

The 2-Stitch X

This is worked the same as the 3-Stitch X (page 68) except you use 2/1 crossings instead of 3/1 crossings. The center of the X is a 2/2L.

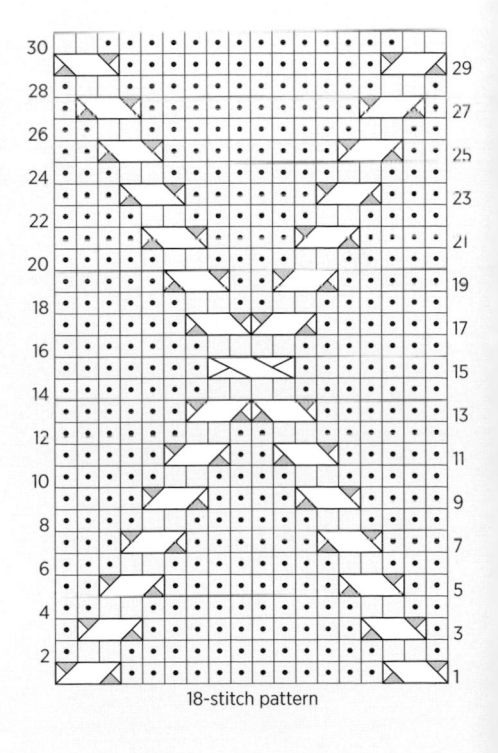

18-stitch pattern

The 1-Stitch X

The traveling stitch X in this swatch is made with 1/1LP crossings and 1/1RP crossings with a 1/1L at the center.

The 1-Stitch X

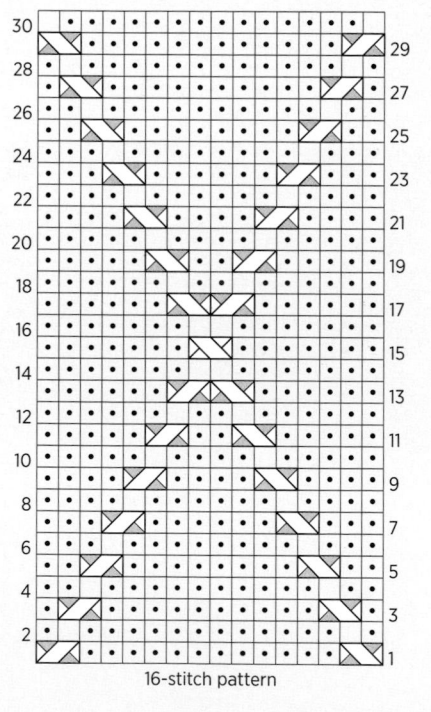

16-stitch pattern

Enlarged X

This is an enlarged version of the 3-Stitch X shown on page 68. Continuing the pattern, 6 rows have been added to the bottom and top of the original X.

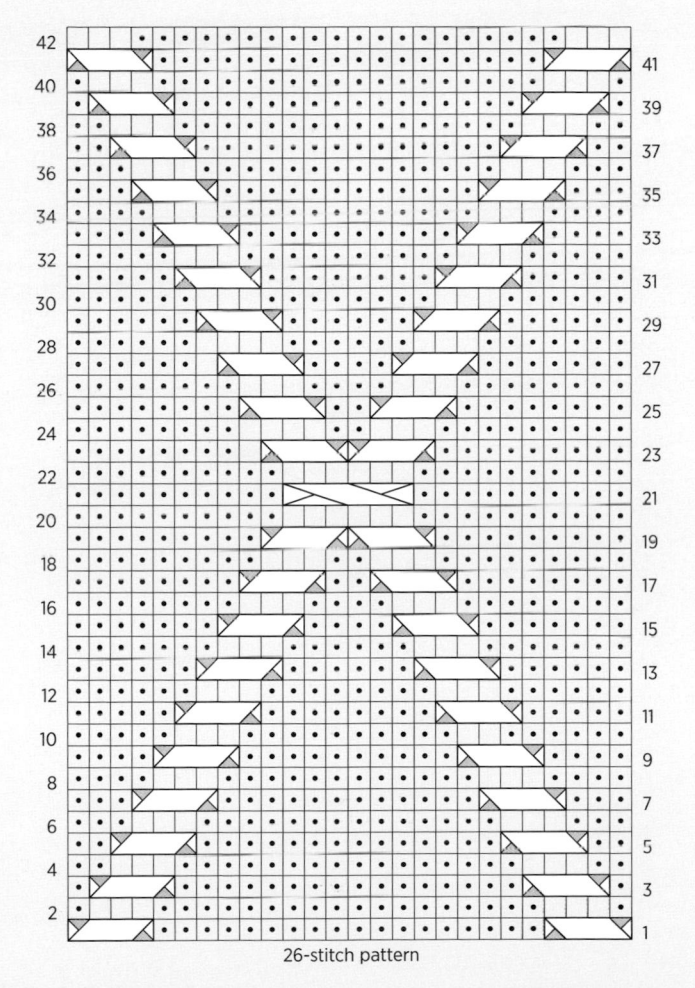

26-stitch pattern

Enlarged X

The Acute X

Making a Sharper Angle

It is possible to make an X pattern with sharper angles by using 3/2 crossings instead of 3/1 crossings. However, this will distort and condense the fabric a bit, so take this into account before using it with other cable patterns. A 3/3L is worked at the center in this sample.

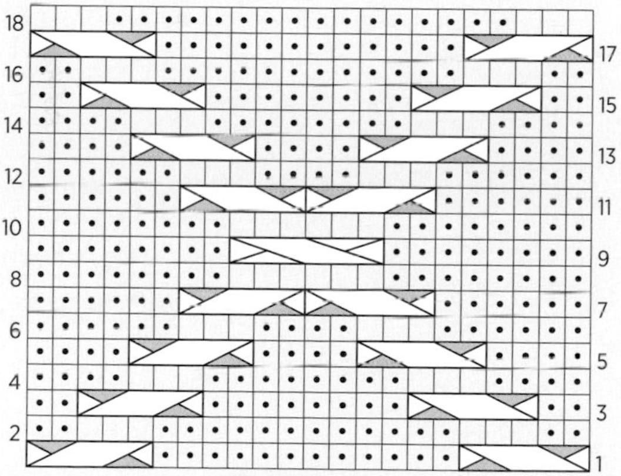

22-stitch pattern

Diagonal Grid

Here a series of 2/1LP crosses makes a diagonal wale fabric. Note the changes in pattern on the right side of the chart in Rows 1–12 and 22–24 in preparation for a new cable, and on the left side of the chart in Rows 9 and 10 and 21 and 22 when a cable has been completed.

Diagonal Grid

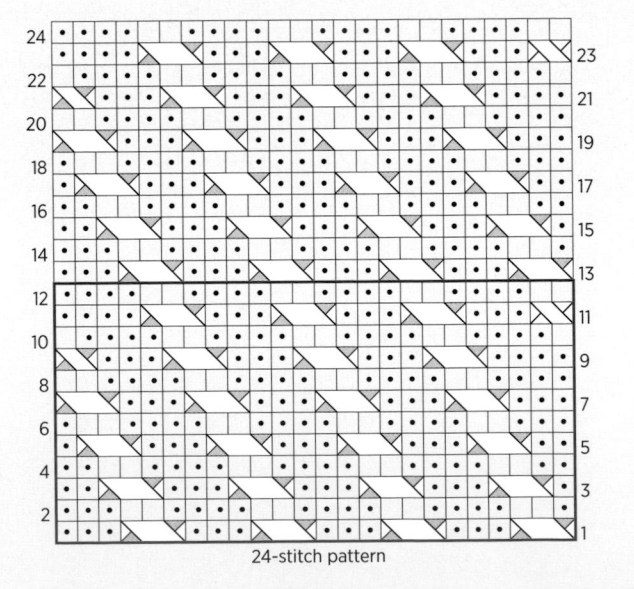

24-stitch pattern

DIAMONDS

Combining right and left crosses that begin at a center point, working outward, then going back to the center point will produce diamond patterns. Here are seven ways to fashion cable diamonds.

Simple Symmetrical Diamond

This diamond begins with a 6-stitch left-cross 3/3L; then the 3 stitches on the right are worked with 3/1RP crosses, while those on the left are worked with 3/1LP crosses. The cables are worked outward until there are 12 background stitches between them; then the crossings are reversed to return to the center.

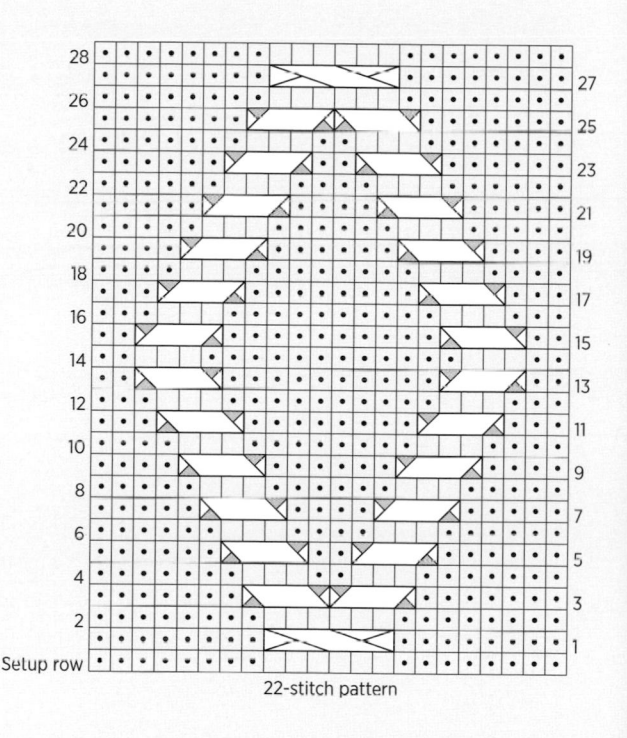

22-stitch pattern

Simple Symmetrical Diamond

Diamond Crossing Variations

There are several different ways to treat the places where the cable parts join in the center. Here are three.

Right-Crossing Diamond

This 18-row diamond uses 2/1RP and 2/1LP crossings with a 2/2R crossing in the center. A Left-Crossing Diamond pattern can be worked by using 2/2L at the center.

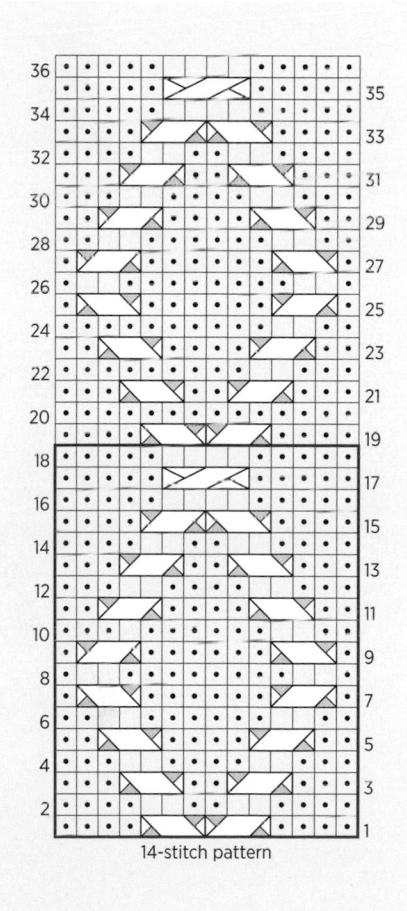

14-stitch pattern

Right-Crossing Diamond

Wrapped-Crossing Diamond

This swatch shows diamonds joined with wrapped stitches. The 4 stitches that are crossed in the previous example are wrapped with the working yarn.

Making the Wrap

1 With yarn in back, slip 4 stitches onto cable needle, and hold in front.

2 *Bring working yarn behind the 4 stitches, then in front of the 4 stitches; repeat from * once more.

3 Bring the working yarn to the back.

4 Knit the 4 stitches.

Completed.

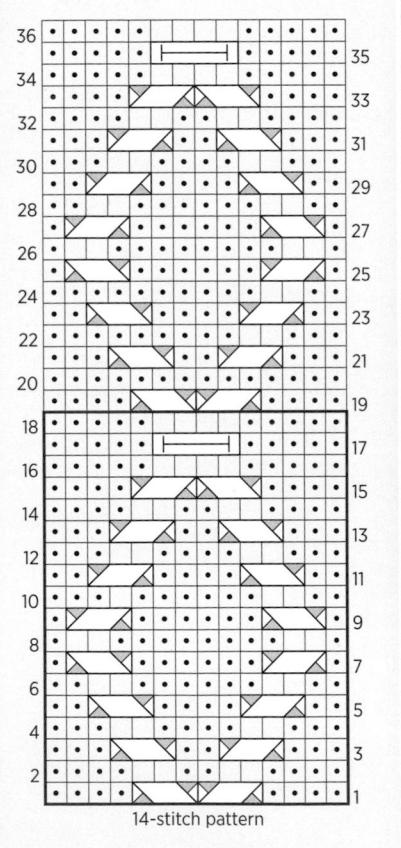

14-stitch pattern

Wrapped-Crossing Diamond

No-Cross Diamond

Another alternative is to work no cross at all. Simply work plain rows where you might have worked a 2/2 crossing or a wrapped join.

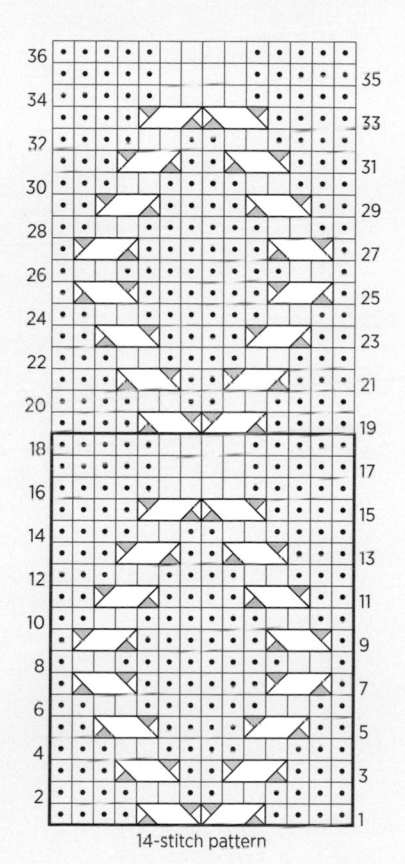

14-stitch pattern

No-Cross Diamond

Diamonds Large and Small

Another way to use diamond cables is to combine large and small cables in a continuous vertical pattern. Here a 14-row diamond transitions to a 26-row diamond and back again.

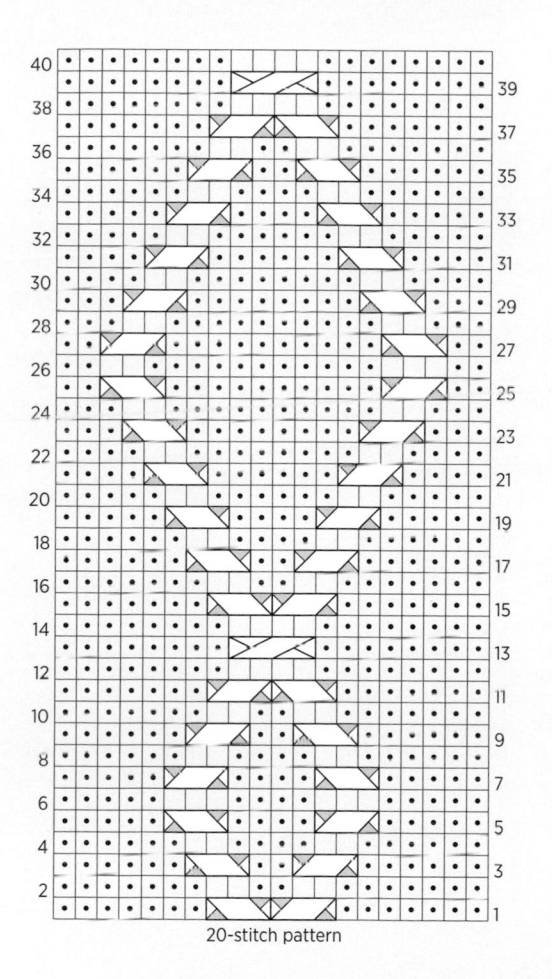

20-stitch pattern

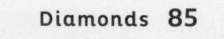

Large and Small Diamonds

Diamond with Rope Cables

A very effective design results from combining a simple rope cable with a diamond. This pattern starts with a 3/3R cable, then transitions to a 24-row diamond, then back again.

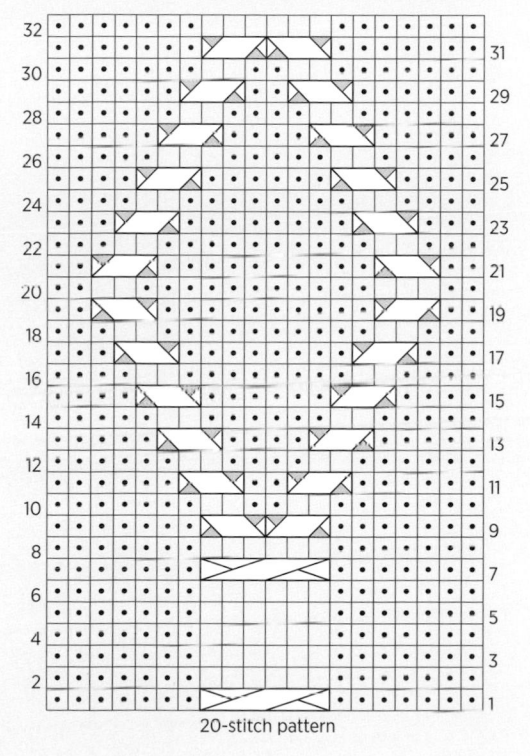

20-stitch pattern

Diamond with Rope Cables

Stand-Alone or Closed Ring Diamond

You may want to work a diamond that stands alone, meaning one that is not worked in a continuous vertical pattern. Because it begins in a field of reverse stockinette stitch, you'll need to increase stitches to start the cable, then decrease them when you've finished. In chapter 7, you'll find more information about compensating for cable take-up and splay. See the symbol chart on page 20 in chapter 1 for an explanation of the increases and decreases used.

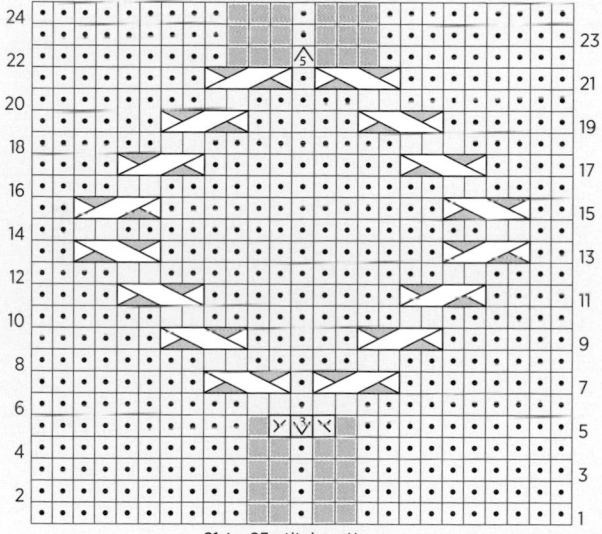

21-to-25-stitch pattern

Stand-Alone Diamond

CURVES AND CIRCLES

These cable patterns are worked essentially the same way as the diamonds, but the combination of crossing types and stitch count makes them a bit curvy, without sharp angles. For example, when working a diamond, at the halfway point you might change direction by switching from a 2/1R to a 2/1L with one plain (wrong-side) row between. When forming circles, working 3 plain (2 wrong side and 1 right side) rows before reversing direction will soften the angle into a curve.

Simple Curves

This example uses two cable ribs, 3/2RP and 3/2LP, that start together at the center, move away from each other, then move back toward each other again to the center. Note that this is the same idea as the No-Cross Diamond on page 82, but the 3/2 crosses produce a softer shape.

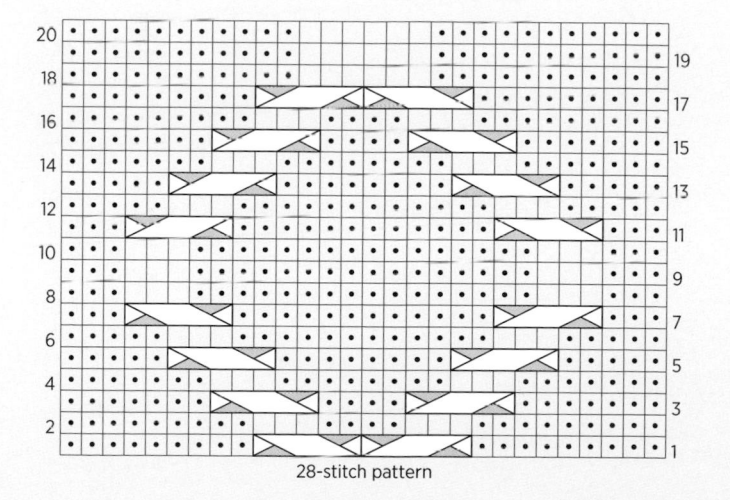

28-stitch pattern

Simple Curves

Curves and Circles **91**

Disc Cables

This variation uses single stockinette stitches crossing 3 purl background stitches or 1/3LP and 1/3RP. There are 6 repeating rows within the discs and 4 repeating rows between the crossings.

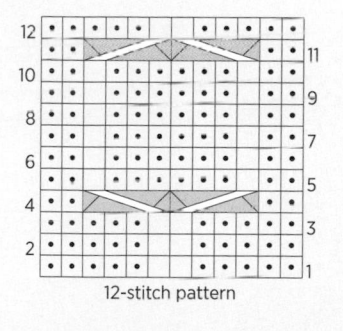

12-stitch pattern

Disc Cables

Squiggles

A series of 2-stitch stockinette cables moving over a reverse stockinette stitch background produce these graceful squiggly lines. Working 2/2LP and 2/2RP crossings produces softer curves than would 2/1LP and 2/1RP crossings.

Squiggles

28-stitch pattern

Multidirectional Squiggle

This pattern makes use of increases and decreases and 3/1, 3/2, and 3/3 right and left purl crossings. It's quite complex in construction but not difficult to produce. See the charts on pages 15–21 of chapter 1 for an explanation of the stitches used.

Multidirectional Squiggle

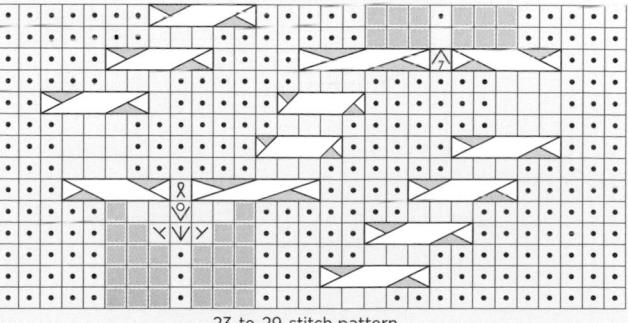

23-to-29-stitch pattern

Stand-Alone or Closed Ring Circle

This pattern uses increases and decreases in a similar way to the Stand-Alone Diamond on page 88. The circle is formed by combining 3/3, 3/2, and 3/1 right and left purl crossings.

Stand-Alone Circle

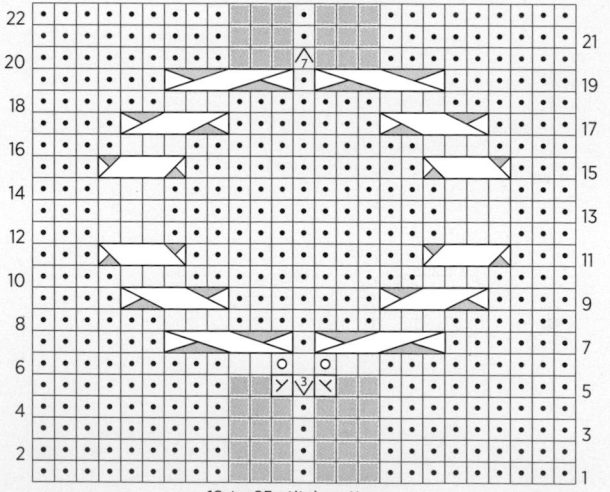

19-to-25-stitch pattern

Quatrefoil

I found this wonderful pattern in Barbara Walker's *Charted Knitting Designs*, though I've seen similar patterns elsewhere. You could tweak this design by making the lines thicker (3-stitch instead of 2-stitch) or making the circles larger or smaller, but it would require some calculating.

Quatrefoil

37-to-49-stitch pattern

CHAPTER 4

Braids and Pretzels

I've looked through a lot of books with cable patterns over the years, and I've seen patterns referred to as "braids" and "pretzels." Many of these patterns look similar, and I'm not exactly sure how they get assigned to one category over the other. For the purpose of this book, I've made a distinction that I hope makes sense.

BRAIDS

These patterns are intertwined, repetitive at even intervals, and symmetrical. They are similar to what we associate with braids of hemp, hair, or other strands — cables, or ribs, are moved over and under each other in a continuing pattern. Braids are also often called plaits.

3-Rib All-Knit Braid

3-Rib All-Knit Braid

This braid consists of 9 stockinette stitches worked into 3 ribs woven together on a background of reverse stockinette stitch. In this pattern 3/3L and 3/3R crosses are alternated between the first 6 stitches and the last 6 stitches every fourth row.

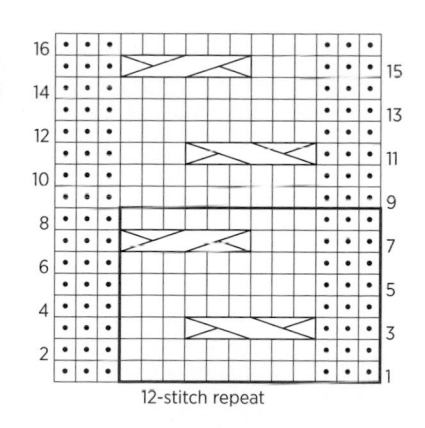

12-stitch repeat

3-Rib Knit and Purl Braid

This braid also consists of 9 stitches worked into 3 ribs, but the crossings are a combination of 2/1LP and 2/1RP crosses with 2/2R crosses. The purl stitches make this braid appear "looser" than the previous one of all knit stitches.

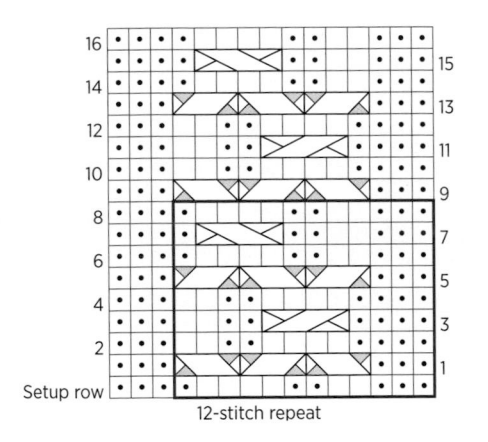

16
15
14
13
12
11
10
9
8
7
6
5
4
3
2
1
Setup row

12-stitch repeat

3-Rib Knit and Purl Braid

4-Rib Knit and Purl Braid

Like the previous braid, this one uses crossings of 2/1RP and 2/1LP crosses with 2/2R and 2/2L crosses. But this braid has 4 ribs, and the first row of the repeat has a 2/1/2RP and the ninth row has a 2/1/2LP. The braid is more complex than the previous two examples.

4-Rib Knit and Purl Braid

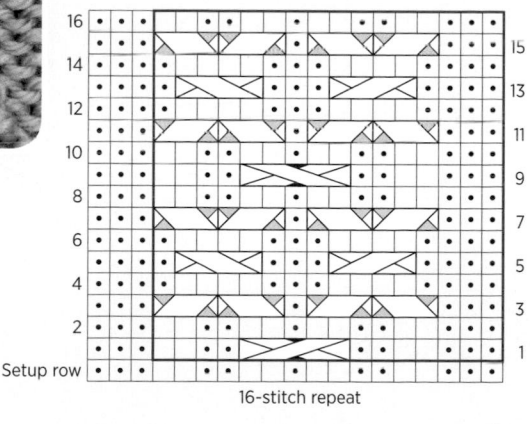

16-stitch repeat

Tight 5-Rib Braid

From here through page 107 is a series of three braids that appear in Barbara Walker's *A Second Treasury of Knitting Patterns*. They show how to create three very different-looking braids from the same basic structure. The first example is a 10-stitch braid that uses side-by-side 2/2L crossings worked on the last 8 stitches, alternating with side-by-side 2/2R crossings worked on the first 8 stitches. The result is a dense and complex braid.

Tight 5-Rib Braid

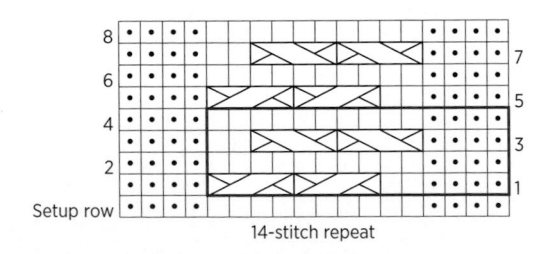

14-stitch repeat

Loose 5-Rib Braid

This pattern changes the previous 5-rib braid by using the 2/1/2P crossings separated by 1 purl stitch in place of side-by-side 2/2 crossings. Like the previous braid, it features 2 right crossings worked on the last set of braid stitches followed by 2 left crossings on the first set of braid stitches, but here there is a purl stitch between the crossings. The result is a looser, more open braid than the previous one.

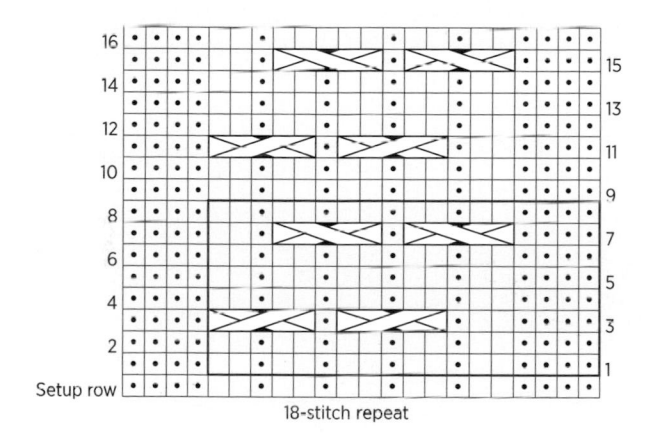

18-stitch repeat

Loose 5-Rib Braid

Elongated 5-Rib Braid

This braid is exactly like the Loose 5-Rib Braid (page 104), except that it has a 10-row repeat rather than 8 rows — there are 2 extra rows between each set of right-, then left-crossing cables. This stretches the braid, and the technique can come in handy if you're trying to combine the braid with another 10-, 20-, or 30-row pattern.

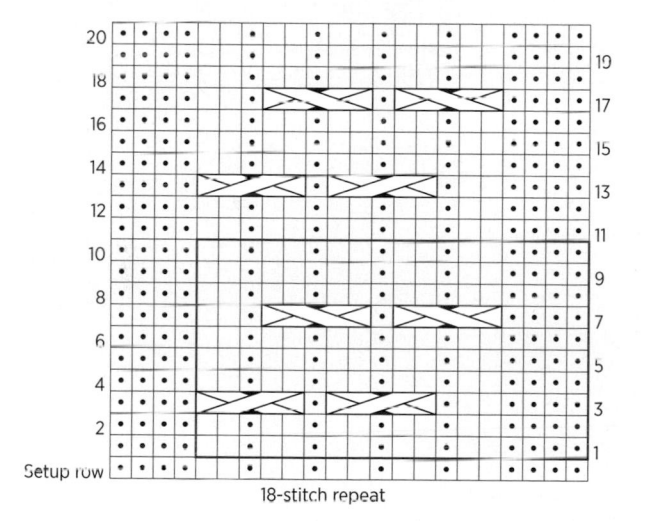

18-stitch repeat

Elongated 5-Rib Braid

6-Rib Braid

Here is a braid worked from a knit 3, purl 1 rib. Like the previous braids, it uses right crossings alternating with left crossings every fourth row. The crossings are 3/1/3 with a neutral purl stitch in the center. The pattern begins with one central crossing; moves out to two, then three crossings; and back to two, then one.

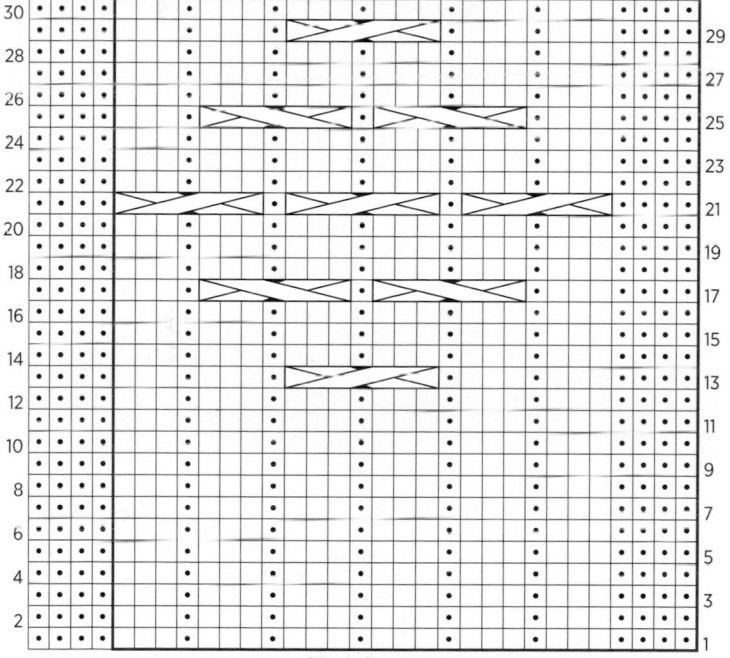

27-stitch repeat

6-Rib Braid

PRETZELS

Unlike braids, the strands or ribs of what I'll call "pretzels" can act quite independently of each other while crossing at regular intervals. The number of ribs may be more than is typical for braids, and the pattern may be asymmetrical, only becoming symmetrical when repeated.

4-Rib Symmetrical Pretzel

This pattern consists of both 2/1RP and 2/1LP crossings, along with 2/2R and 2/2L crossings where the ribs meet. It is both symmetrical and graceful.

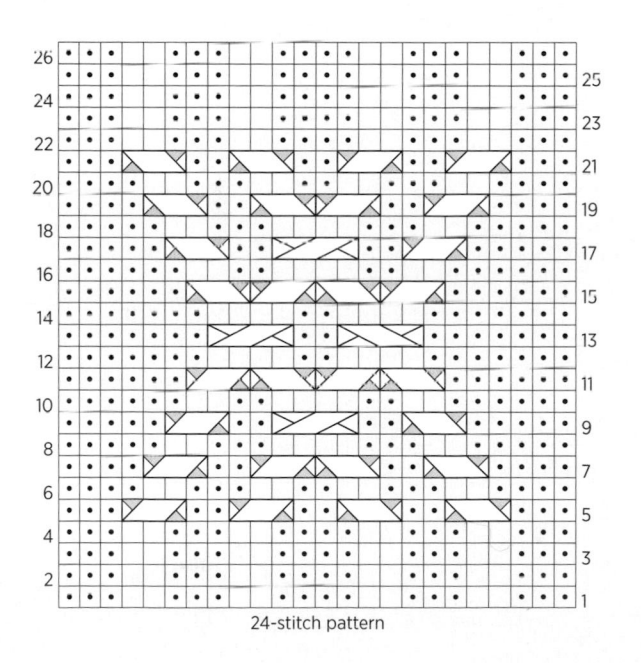

24-stitch pattern

4-Rib Symmetrical Pretzel

4-Rib Asymmetrical Pretzel

Like the previous 4-rib pretzel, this one uses both 2/1RP and
2/1LP crossings, along with 2/2R and 2/2L crossings where the
ribs meet. But it also uses crossings of 2/2RP and 2/2LP and
elongated ribs on the left side of the lower pattern and the right
side of the upper pattern to create the asymmetry.

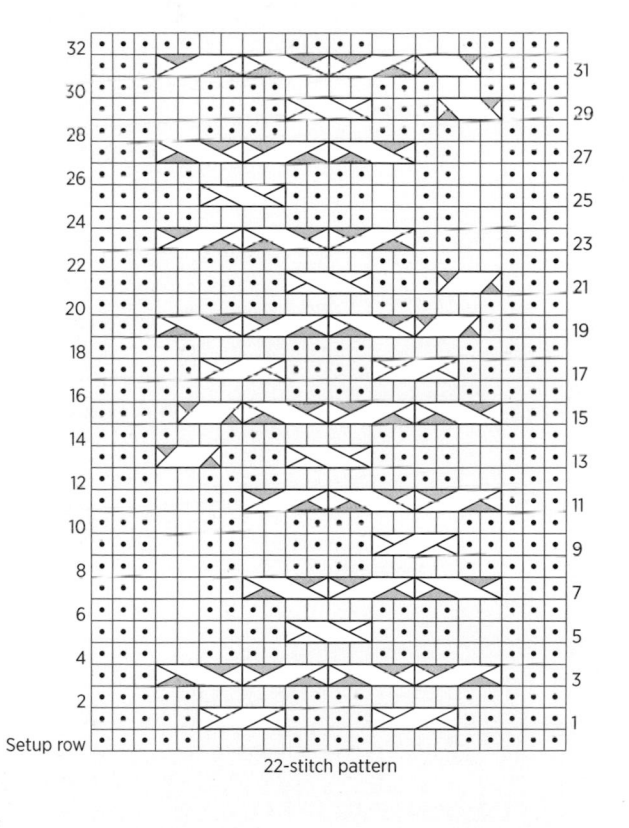

22-stitch pattern

4-Rib Asymmetrical Pretzel

5-Rib Pretzel

Here's a wonderfully complex 5-rib pretzel that has 1 stationary rib in the center and 4 outer ribs that seem to grow from and return to the same base. The meeting of the ribs in the center between the two repeats shown in this swatch forms a small braid.

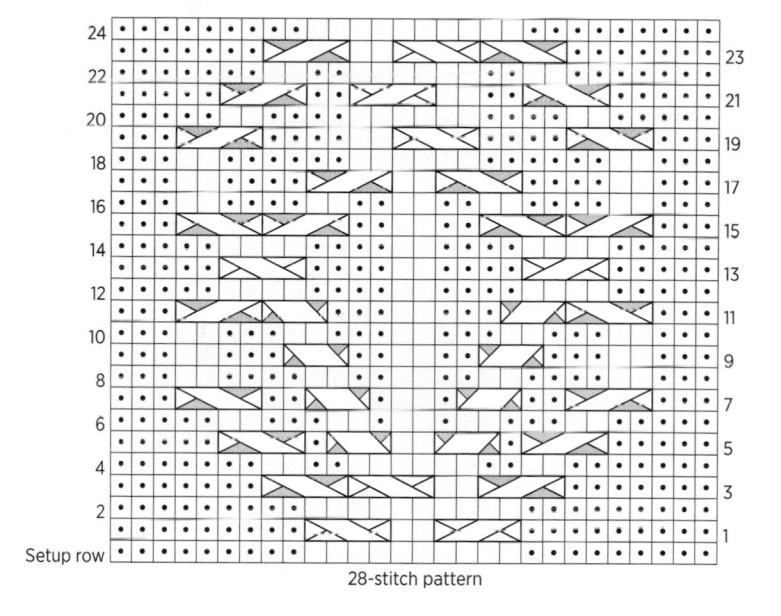

28-stitch pattern

5-Rib Pretzel

6-Rib Pretzel

This 6-rib pretzel uses six different crossings: 2/2RP, 2/2LP, 2/2R, 2/2L, 2/1RP, and 2/1LP. The structure is very braidlike in the way the ribs move over and under each other, but I've categorized it as a pretzel because of its openness.

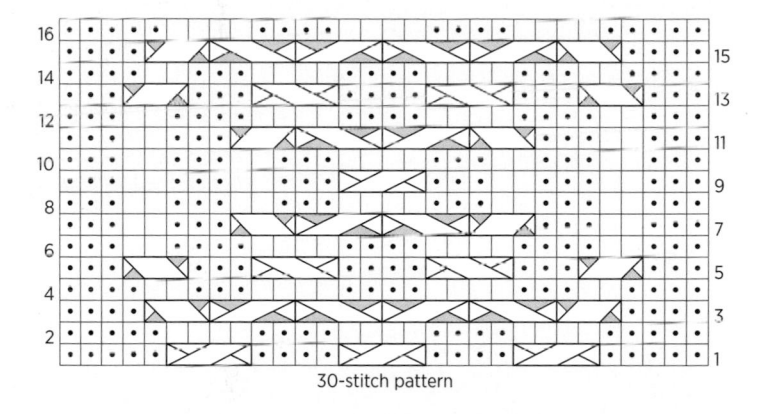

30-stitch pattern

6-Rib Pretzel

8-Rib Pretzel

This design is different from all the others in this chapter in that its ribs begin as 2/2LP and 2/2RP crossings, then go to 2/1LP and 2/1RP crossings, and finally are down to 1/1RP and 1/1LP crossings. The result is an intricate lattice pattern that is lighter, or less bulky, than the others. Note that this pattern also requires increases and decreases. See chapter 1 for complete explanations of the stitches.

24-to-28-stitch pattern

8-Rib Pretzel

COMBINING BRAIDS AND PRETZELS

There is no limit to the variety and complexity that can be achieved when the various cabling techniques are combined in a design. Here are two examples of braids and pretzels working together. Both are presented in Barbara Walker's *Charted Knitting Designs*.

Double-Knot Cable

This design begins in a pretzel-like fashion with a bonus: The pretzels are linked with 3/3 rope cables as presented in chapter 2. The pattern then moves into a braid at the top. Two repeats are shown in the swatch.

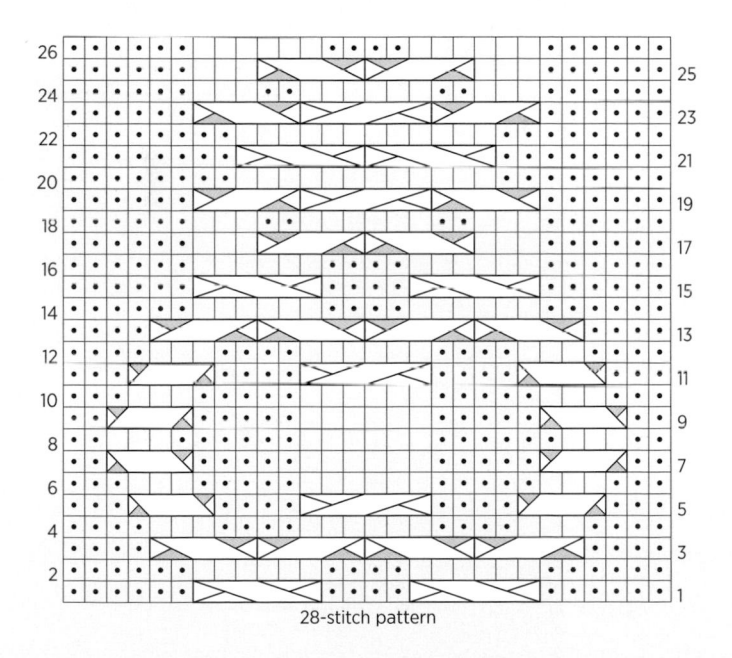

28-stitch pattern

Double-Knot Cable

Baroque Cable

I made a mistake when initially knitting this swatch. On Row 19, I placed two left-crossing cables in the center instead of right-crossing cables. I did not realize this until after I'd finished the swatch. Notice the big difference in the very center of the design between the first swatch with the mistake and the corrected swatch. This is to say we need to pay attention when working cable crossings! (The chart for this pattern is on page 124.)

Incorrect Cable Crossing

Baroque Cable

42-stitch pattern

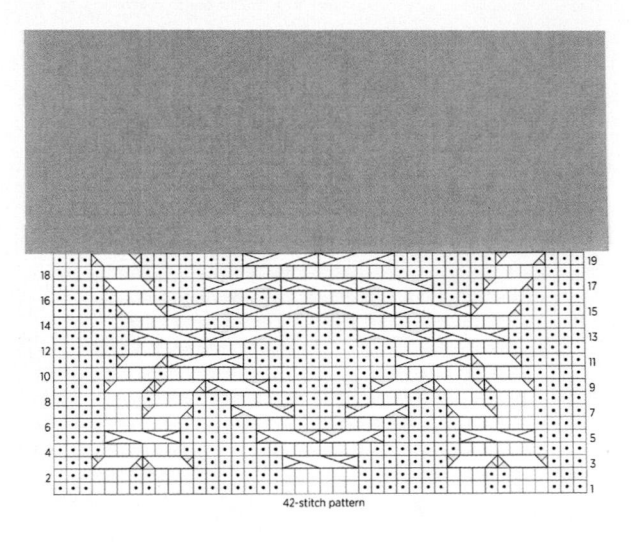

42-stitch pattern

Following a Large Chart

It's very easy to lose your place when following a large and complicated chart. A good solution is to mark the current row with a straight edge of some sort. I find that it's best to block the rows above the current row — it's okay to see what you've already knitted, but distracting to be looking at what comes next. In this photo, a piece of cardstock is used to track the rows, and here you are ready to follow the chart to work Row 19.

CHAPTER 5

Fillers, Ribbings, and Allover Patterns

When designing a cabled garment or other item, panels of simple stitches come in handy as a way to showcase the cables or to provide a simple pattern where shaping occurs. It's also usual to place a ribbing at the lower end of a garment and at the cuffs. Finally, you may want to knit with an allover pattern, one that is not divided into panels of distinct cable patterns and fillers.

FILLERS

Bands of simple stitches can be used in the areas where shaping happens in a sweater, such as the armholes of the body and the cap and underarm of the sleeves. They provide a plain ground into which you can increase or decrease as necessary without interrupting a cable pattern. They can also be knit in panels between more elaborate cabled panels. Here are a few options.

Seed Stitch

Seed Stitch

Seed stitch is an easy-to-knit filler that can be worked on an even or an odd number of stitches, in the round or back and forth. You simply work alternating single knits and purls in the rows, and you work a knit stitch above a purl stitch and vice versa in each subsequent row. It is ideal for areas requiring shaping.

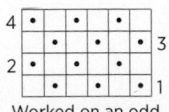

Worked on an odd or even number of stitches.

Moss Stitch

Moss stitch is worked the same as seed stitch except that you work 2 rows the same, then work knits above purls and purls above knits. As with seed stitch, it is ideal for areas requiring shaping.

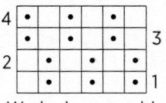

Worked on an odd or even number of stitches.

Moss Stitch

Double Seed Stitch

Double seed stitch, also called double moss and box stitch, works like seed and moss stitch except that you work 2 stitches *and* 2 rows the same. Although it is worked on a multiple of 4 stitches, you can easily increase or decrease to a different number of stitches and maintain the pattern.

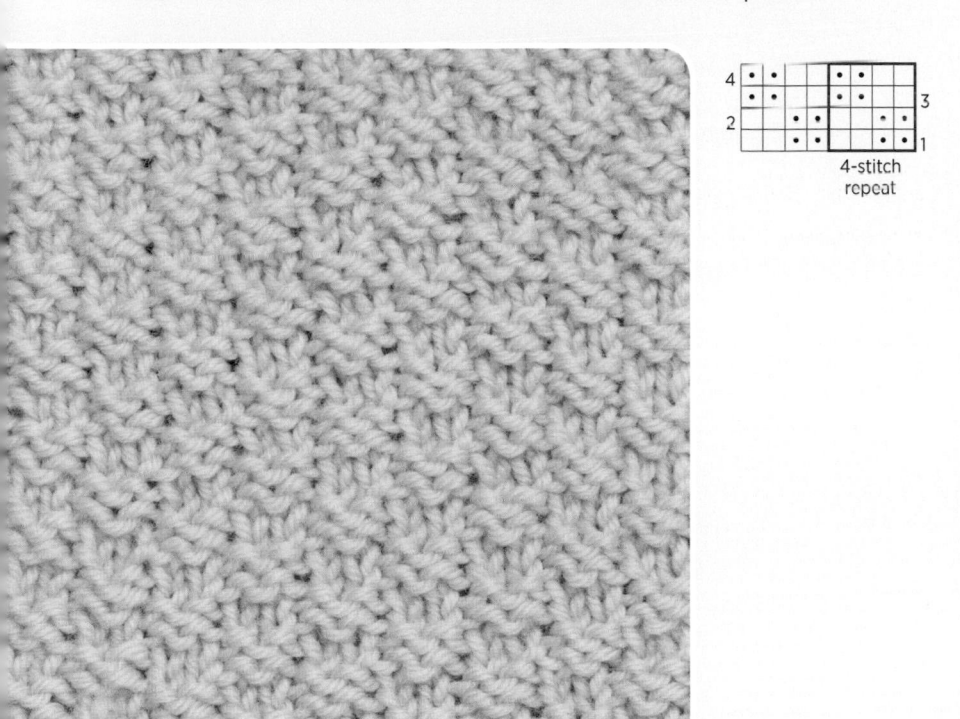

Double Seed Stitch

Honeycomb Stitch

This is a somewhat dense stitch that's more suited as a decorative panel than as a ground for shaping. It is a very easy-to-remember pattern and works up quickly, in spite of the need to make a crossing with each stitch every fourth row.

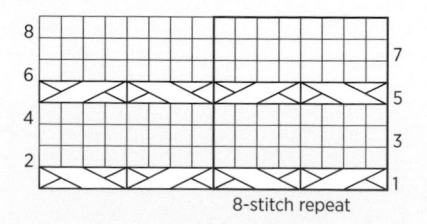

Honeycomb Stitch

8-stitch repeat

Mini-Honeycomb Stitch

Mini-Honeycomb Stitch

Here's a condensed version of the Honeycomb Stitch (page 131). To speed up the knitting, you can use the 1/1R and 1/1L no-cable-needle method to form the crossings instead of moving stitches onto a cable needle. See page 32 for details.

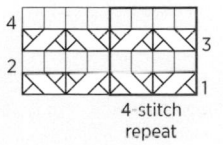

4-stitch repeat

Trinity Stitch

This is a hugely popular stitch in Aran sweater knitting. It's difficult to chart this stitch accurately, so I'm giving you the row-by-row instructions as well. The stitch is worked on a multiple of 4 stitches, and you make 3 stitches from 1, followed by 1 stitch from 3 across wrong-side rows. Trinity stitch is well suited to decorative panels.

Trinity Stitch

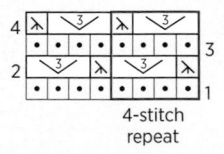

Trinity Stitch

ROW 1 (RS): Purl.

ROW 2 (WS): *(K1, p1, k1) in same stitch, p3tog; repeat from * to end of row.

ROW 3: Purl.

ROW 4: *P3 tog, (k1, p1, k1) in same stitch; repeat from * to end of row.

Tight Lattice Stitch

This stitch has a tightly woven appearance. Like the previous few stitches, it is best used for decorative panels not requiring shaping. Although it's worked with a 4-stitch repeat, you need to start with at least 8 stitches.

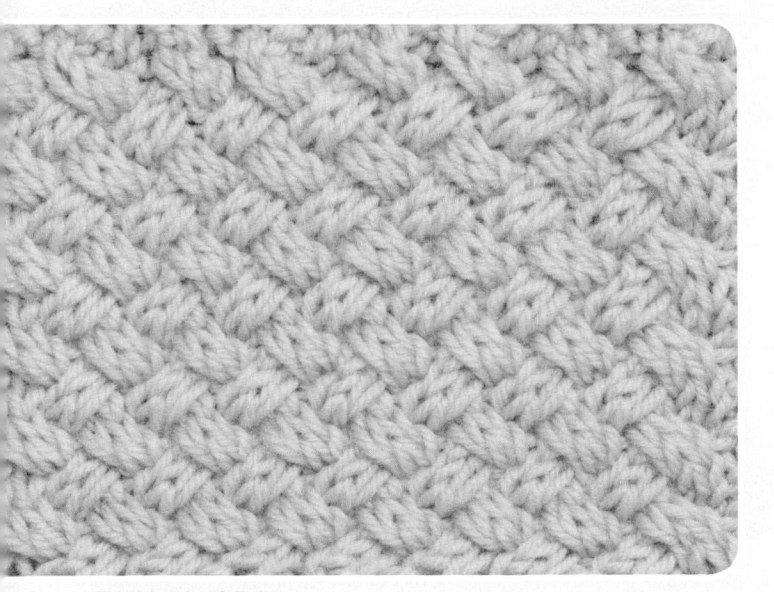

Tight Lattice Stitch

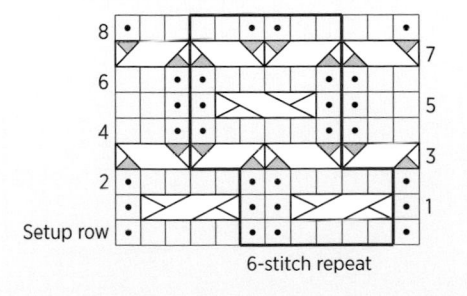

8
6
4
2
Setup row

7
5
3
1

6-stitch repeat

Woven-Basket Lattice Stitch

This stitch combines elements of the Honeycomb Stitch (page 131) and Lattice Stitch (facing page) with a few purls added for spacing. Worked on a multiple of 6 stitches plus 2, it makes a highly decorative panel and could also be used as an allover pattern stitch.

Woven-Basket Lattice Stitch

Worked on 6 + 8 stitches.

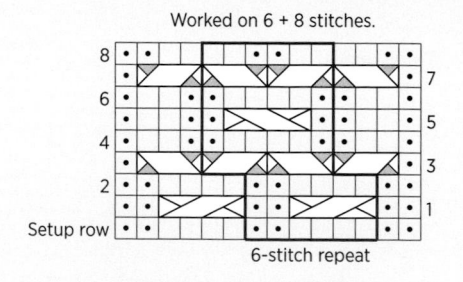

6-stitch repeat

RIBBINGS

As previously mentioned, ribbing is often used at the bottom of sweaters and at the cuffs of sleeves. In addition to standard knit 1, purl 1 or knit 2, purl 2 ribbings that work great with cables, here are a few decorative options. You can easily make up your own — just be sure you combine columns of knit patterns with columns of plain purls so you get the necessary elasticity.

Mini-Cable Ribbing

A 1/1L cable converts the standard knit 2, purl 2 rib into a decorative rib.

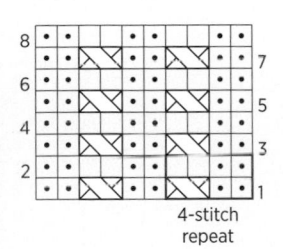

4-stitch repeat

Mini-Cable Ribbing

Ribbing Plus Cables

Here we use the knit 2, purl 2 ribbing technique, but we add a column with 2/2 cables. You can choose to turn the cables to the left as shown or to the right. *Note:* A 4-stitch cable is approximately the same width as 2 knit stitches.

Ribbing and Cables

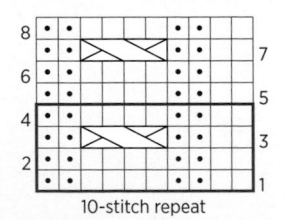

10-stitch repeat

Double-Crossed Cable Ribbing

This pattern pairs columns of 2 purl stitches with 4-stitch cables where the 2 outer stitches each cross the 2 center stitches, one from right to left, the other from left to right. The cable is easily adaptable to 5 or more stitches — simply cross the 2 outer stitches over all the center stitches.

Double-Crossed Cable Ribbing

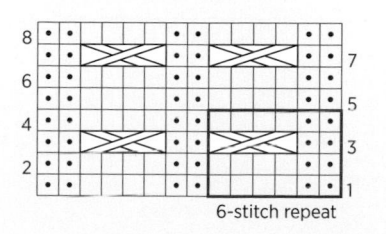

6-stitch repeat

Floating Zigzag Ribbing

The zigzag cable uses 1/2 cables turned on every right-side row, alternating between 1/2L and 1/2R. The zigzag is flanked by single stockinette stitches, and there are columns of 2 purl stitches between.

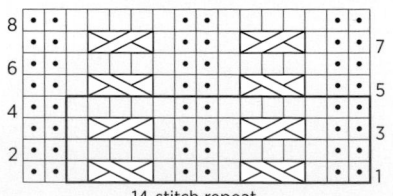

Floating Zigzag Ribbing

14-stitch repeat

Squiggles and Twists

When you knit into the back of a stitch on right-side rows and purl into the back of the same stitch on wrong-side rows, you get a very tight, narrow column of twisted knit stitches. In this sample the twisted stitches flank alternating rows of 1/1R, 1/1L and 1/1L, 1/1R. This is a wonderful accent for cable knitting and can be used anywhere, not just for ribbing.

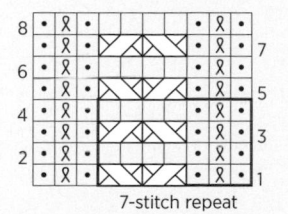

Squiggles and Twists

7-stitch repeat

Hourglass Ribbing

Here we use a 6-stitch version of the Hourglass Cable from chapter 2, page 60, with columns of 4 purl stitches.

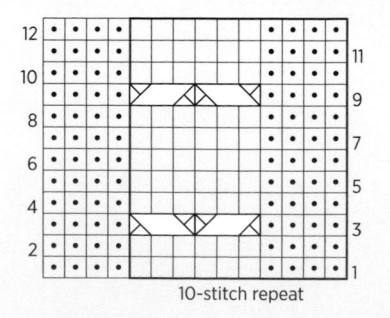

Hourglass Ribbing

10-stitch repeat

ALLOVER PATTERNS

Allover patterns can be used, as the name implies, as the single pattern in an entire garment or other item, or they can be used as wide panels. Allover patterns are usually intertwined, making them unsuitable for working in very narrow panels. This is the case with all of the following samples, except the Banded Cable pattern on page 150.

Lattice with Right Crossings

This allover lattice uses the structure of the Diagonal Grid from chapter 3 (page 75), but it's worked in both directions. In this sample all crossings are made from left to right, and this becomes a feature of the pattern.

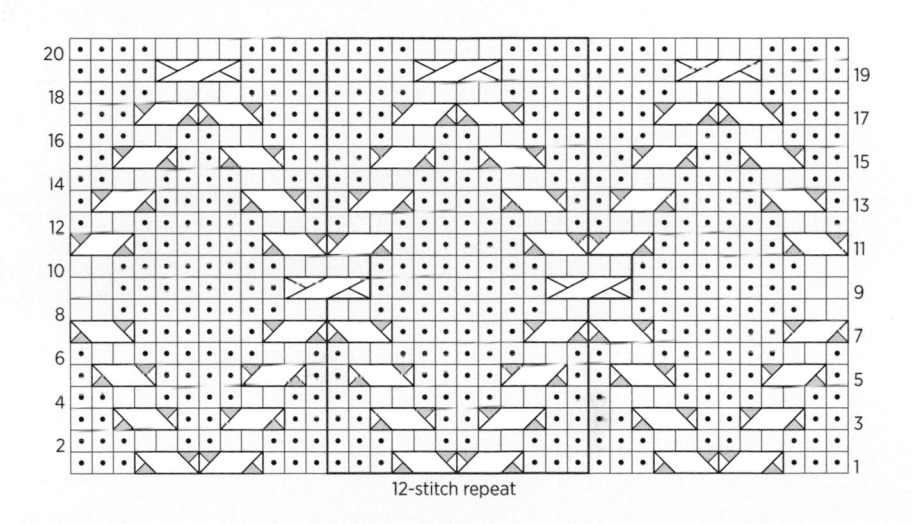

12-stitch repeat

Lattice with Right Crossings

Lattice with Right and Left Crossings

This allover is worked exactly as the previous sample except that the crossings are made in alternating directions. The ribs weave over and under each other, and there is no dominant directional feature.

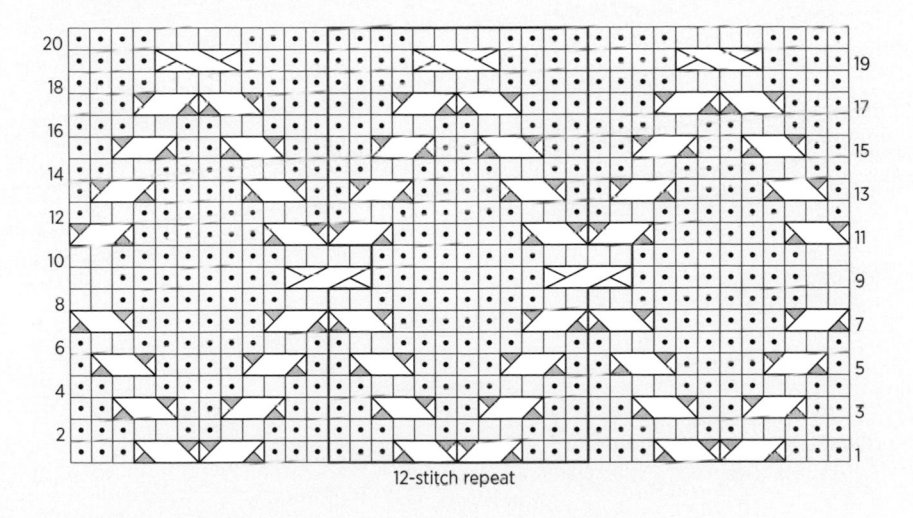

12-stitch repeat

Lattice with Right and Left Crossings

Staggered Diamonds

Staggered Diamonds uses the Diamonds Large and Small cable from chapter 3 (page 84). Stitches from the reverse stockinette stitch background of that pattern are removed to allow the diamonds to nestle.

48-stitch pattern

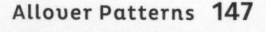

Staggered Diamonds

Staggered Diamonds Variation

You can nestle the diamond cable patterns even closer together by removing more of the background stitches between them.

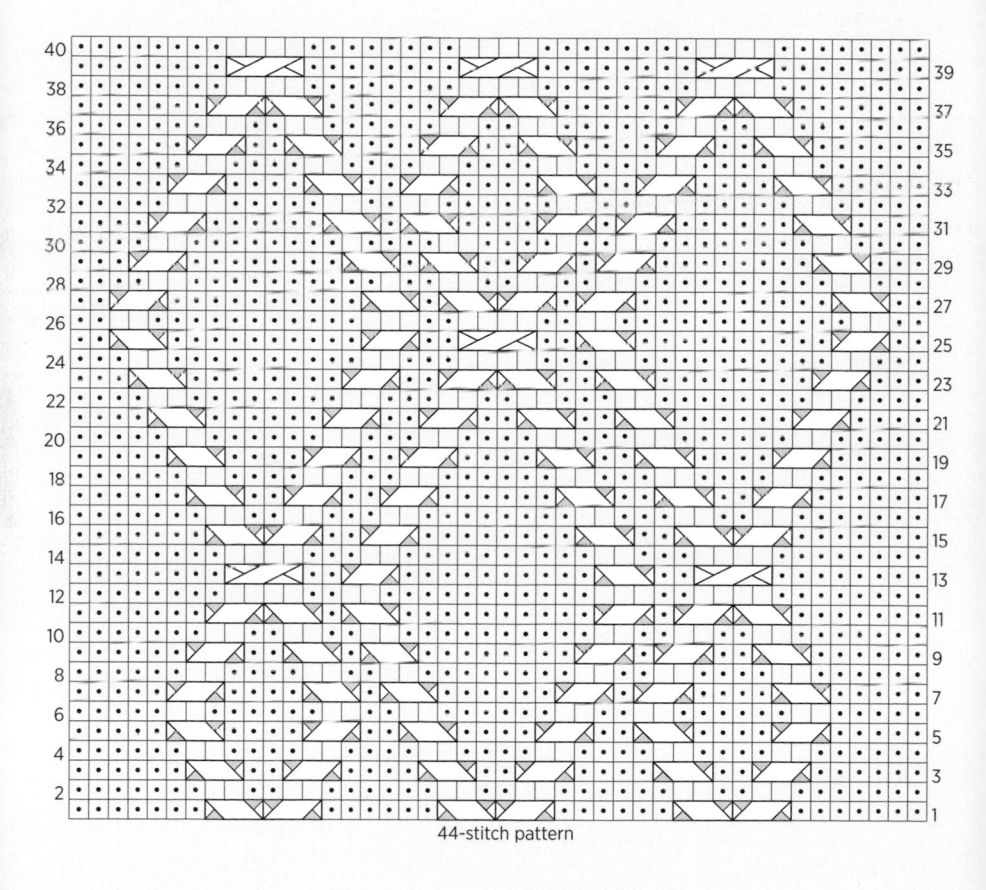

44-stitch pattern

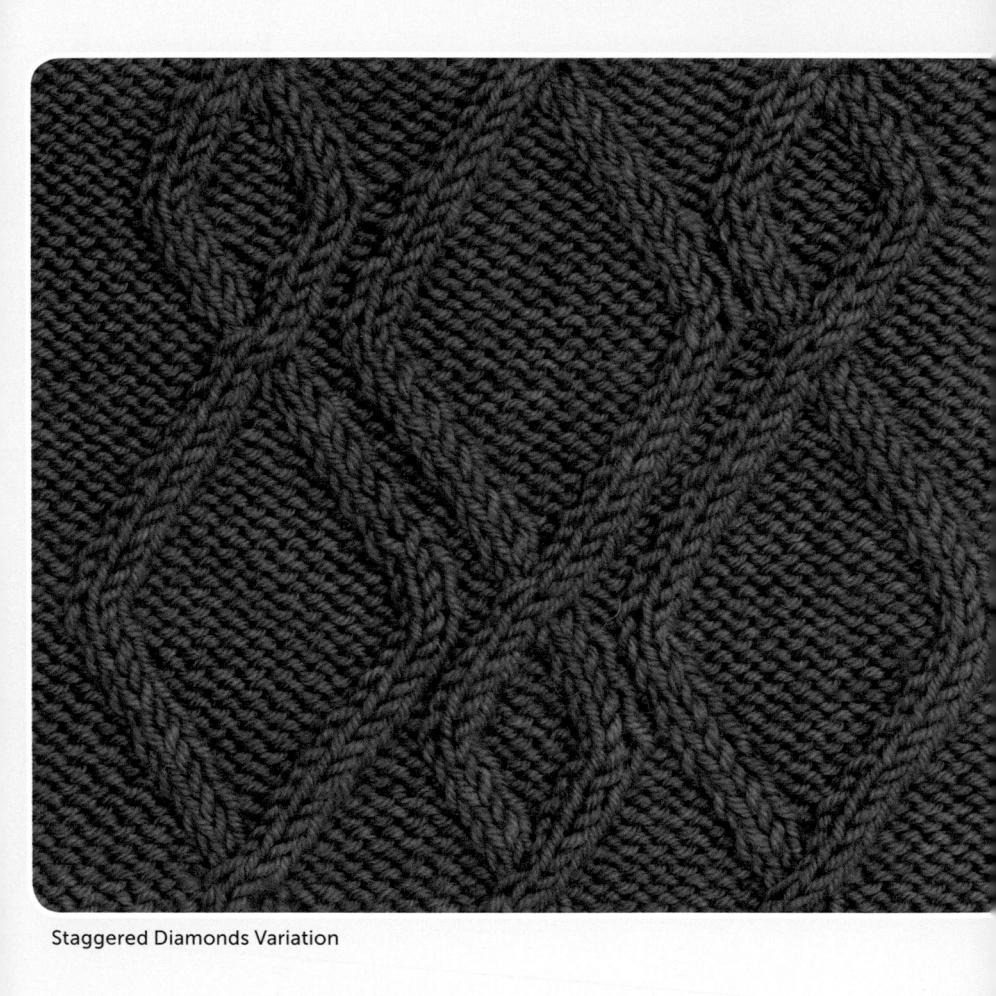

Staggered Diamonds Variation

Banded Cable Pattern

Because there are columns of purl stitches between the cables, this allover pattern could actually be worked as a 14-stitch panel. But I think it works better as an allover. Varied ribbed columns interrupt 6-stitch cables, making the ribs of the cables change from 3 stitches to 2 or 1 stitch.

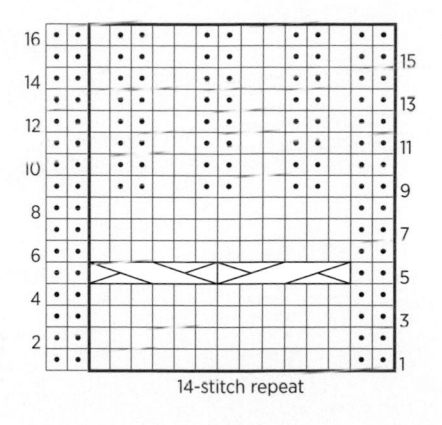

14-stitch repeat

Banded Cable

Braided Cables

Cables and braids are linked together in this allover pattern with a 12-stitch repeat. Three full repeats are shown on the swatch. The pattern uses 2/2R and 2/2L cables with 2/1RP and 2/1LP cables.

Worked on a multiple of 12 + 14 stitches.

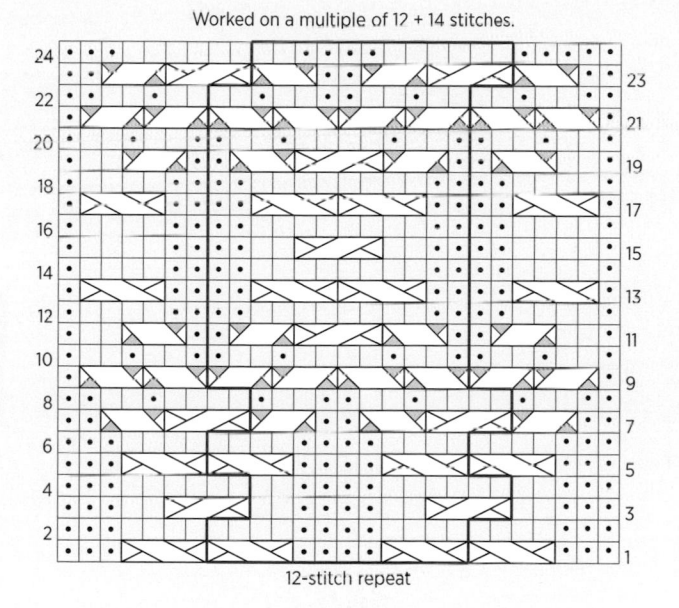

12-stitch repeat

Braided Cables

CHAPTER 6

Dressing Up Your Cables

As if weaving sets of stitches over, under, and around each other doesn't provide enough knitting excitement, here we'll look at ways to add even more interest to your cables. We'll start with texture and bobbles, then move on to color and beads. We'll even take a look at reversible cables.

ADDING TEXTURE AND BOBBLES

The cables presented thus far have been set on a plain background of reverse stockinette stitch. Here we'll look at adding texture to select parts of the background, as well as adding bobbles.

Dressed Diamonds Large and Small: Odd Number of Stitches

This pattern is similar to the Diamonds Large and Small in chapter 3 (page 84), except that this version has an odd number of stitches between the diamond ribs and the other has an even number. There are 2/1/2RP crossings where the cables meet, the large diamond is filled with double seed stitch (page 130), and the small diamond has a bobble in the center. See Bobbles on page 158.

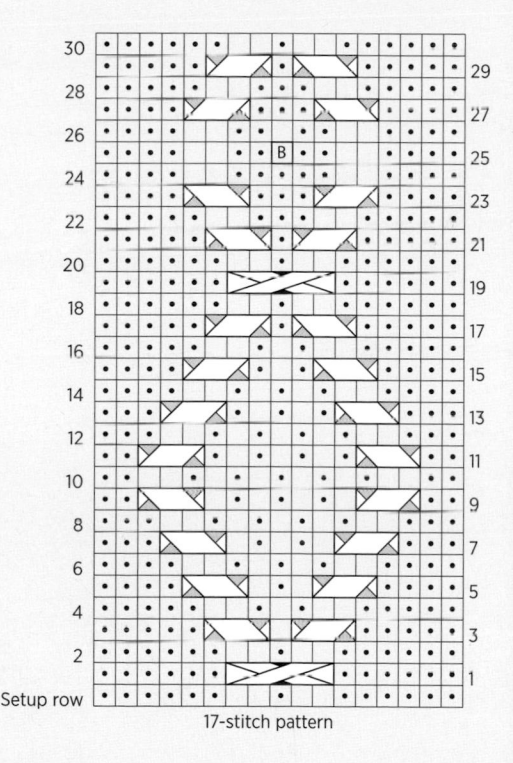

Setup row

17-stitch pattern

Dressed Diamonds: Large and Small
Odd Number of Stitches

Bobbles

Bobbles can be made with 4, 5, or 6 stitches, and they can be worked over 1 to 5 rows. They can be worked in stockinette stitch, reverse stockinette stitch, or seed stitch. Usually you work a bobble into the center of an odd-numbered group of stitches, working the bobble into the center stitch of the group. But you can also work a bobble into the center of an even-numbered group of stitches, working the bobble into the center 2 stitches as if they were one, then restoring the 2 separate stitches. Here are some samples.

Top Row (left to right): Stockinette Stitch Bobbles

BOBBLE 8 (WORKED INTO 2 STITCHES): (K2tog, p1, k1, p1) into same 2 stitches; (turn and purl 1 row, turn and knit 1 row) twice; turn and purl 1 row; turn and ssk, k1, k2tog, pass ssk over both the k1 and k2tog.

BOBBLE 9: (K1, p1) twice into same stitch; turn and purl 1 row; turn and ssk, k2tog, pass ssk over k2tog.

BOBBLE 10: (K1, p1) twice into same stitch; turn and purl 1 row; turn and knit 1 row; turn and purl 1 row; turn and ssk, k2tog, pass ssk over k2tog.

BOBBLE 11: Work as for Bobble 10, but work 5 rows of stockinette stitch instead of 3 rows.

Top row: Bobbles 8, 9, 10, 11

Middle row: Bobbles 5, 6, 7

Bottom row: Bobbles 1, 2, 3, 4

Middle Row (left to right): Reverse Stockinette Stitch Bobbles

BOBBLE 5: (К1, p1) twice into same stitch; (turn and knit 1 row, turn and purl 1 row) twice; turn and knit 1 row; turn and ssk, k2tog, pass ssk over k2tog.

BOBBLE 6: Work as for Bobble 5, but work 3 rows of reverse stockinette stitch instead of 5.

BOBBLE 7: Work as for Bobble 5, but work only 1 row of reverse stockinette stitch.

Bottom Row (left to right): Seed Stitch Bobbles

BOBBLE 1: (К1, p1) twice into same stitch; lift the third, second, and first stitches over the fourth stitch.

BOBBLE 2: (К1, p1) three times into same stitch; turn and work (p1, k1) three times; turn and slip 3 purlwise, k3tog, pass 3 slipped stitches over the k3tog.

BOBBLE 3: (К1, p1) three times into same stitch; turn and work (p1, k1) three times; turn and work (k1, p1) three times; turn and work (p1, k1) three times; turn and slip 3 purlwise, k3tog, pass 3 slipped stitches over the k3tog.

BOBBLE 4: Work as for Bobble 3, but work 5 rows of seed stitch instead of 3 rows.

Dressed Diamonds Large and Small: Even Number of Stitches

Adding a textured background of double seed stitch (page 130) and bobbles to select background areas with an even number of stitches isn't as straightforward as with an odd count; the double seed stitch won't be exactly symmetrical, and there is no center stitch in which to work a bobble. As you see in this sample, the double seed stitch is worked within the diamond without beginning and ending with the same stitch, as in the previous example. But without close scrutiny you can't really tell. In the small diamond the bobble is worked over 2 stitches rather than 1, so it sits directly in the center. See Bobbles on page 158.

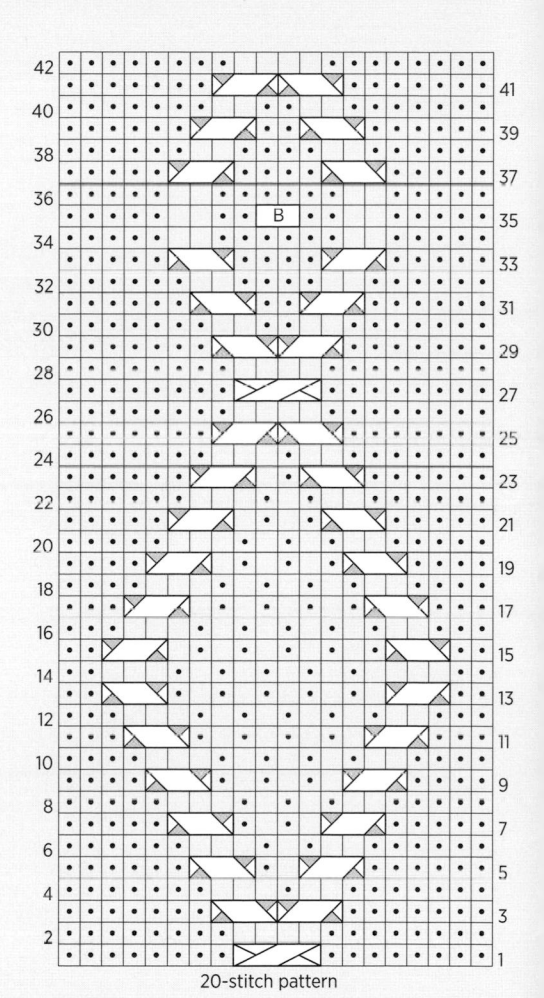

20-stitch pattern

Large and Small
Dressed Diamonds:
Even Number of
Stitches

Bobbles between Diamonds

This diamond pattern has a cluster of bobbles both top and bottom. Note that the diamond ribs don't actually cross, but you'd never know because the bobbles will cover the "join" between diamonds. The interior of the diamond has double seed stitch (page 130) as the background.

Bobbles between Diamonds

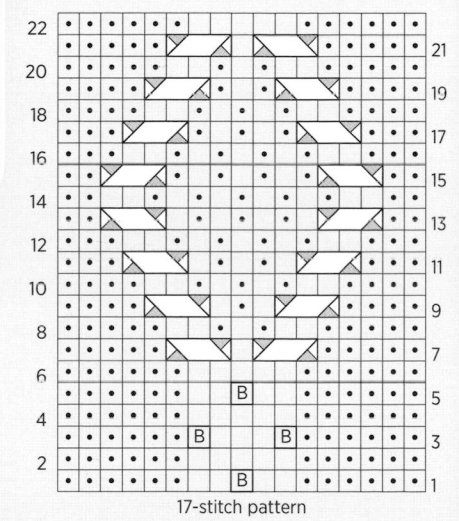

17-stitch pattern

Half Diamond with Bobble Cluster

This swatch shows half of a diamond with bobbles on one side and knit 1, purl 1 rib on the other. You could also make this pattern into a full diamond completely filled with bobbles.

Half Diamond with Bobble Cluster

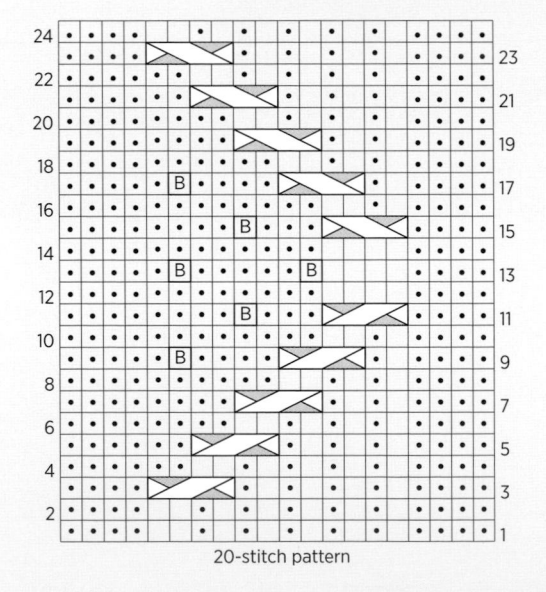

20-stitch pattern

Half-and-Half Textured Rope Cable

A 5/5L rope cable is worked with 5 stitches in stockinette stitch and 5 stitches in seed stitch. The result is a textured strand twining with a plain strand.

Work the shaded stitches in seed stitch pattern.

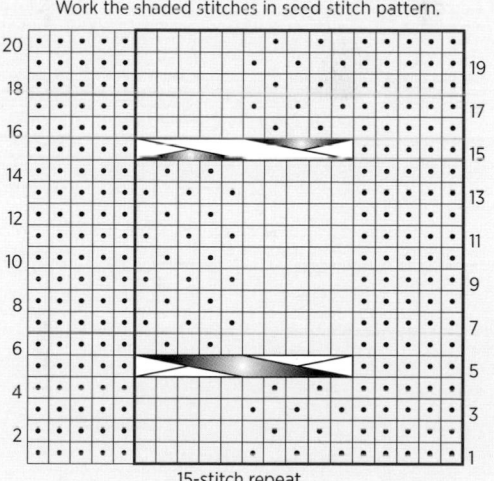

15-stitch repeat

Half-and-Half Textured Rope Cable

Half-and-Half Outward Double Cable

The United Outward Double Cable shown in chapter 2, page 57, is worked here with 3 knit stitches crossing 3 seed stitches to the right, then to the left on Row 3. The seed stitch is worked in the center of Rows 4 through 8; then 3 seed stitches cross 3 knit stitches to the right, then the left.

Half-and-Half Outward Double Cable

Work the shaded stitches in seed stitch pattern.

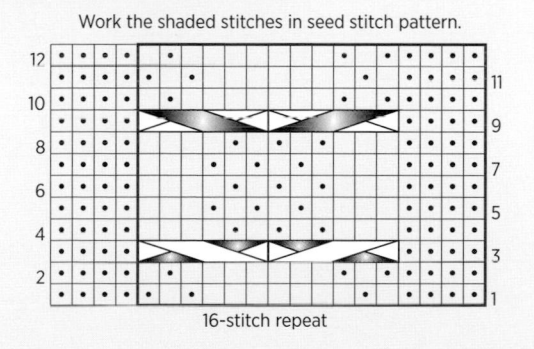

16-stitch repeat

Binding Rope Cables

Another way to add texture to rope cables is to wrap, or bind, the stitches of one-half of the cable. This sample shows a 3/3R cable where 3 of the stitches are bound. See page 21 of chapter 1 for a description of binding.

Binding Rope Cables

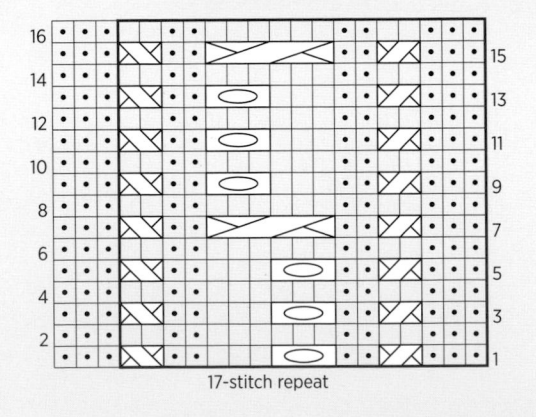

17-stitch repeat

Binding Other Cables

This sample shows binding on all ribs of a 4-rib pretzel, the same as that presented in chapter 4, page 110. The previous sample has a bind-3 stitch; this one uses a bind-2 stitch. See page 21 of chapter 1 for a description of binding.

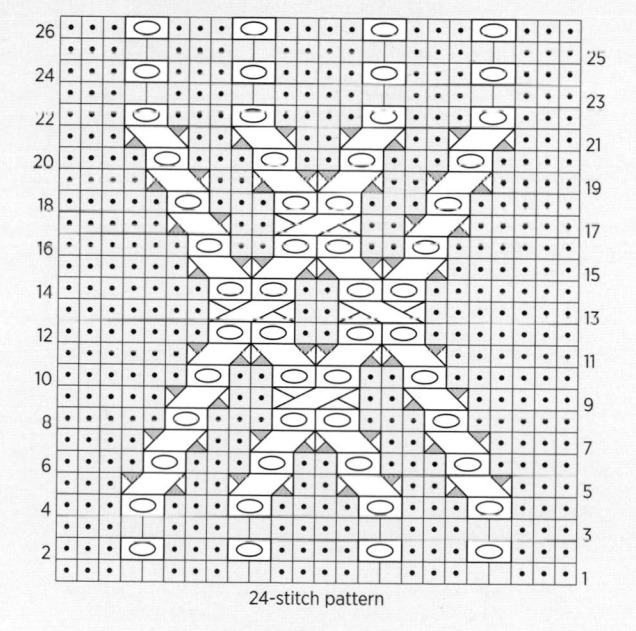

24-stitch pattern

TWO-COLOR CABLES

Working cables in two or more colors is a great way to add interest. Here are five ideas for coloring cables.

Half-and-Half Colored Rope Cable

This is worked like the Half-and-Half Textured Rope Cable on page 164 but with a second color of yarn instead of seed stitch. This example is a 3/3L cross. As with all stranded multicolored knitting, it's important not to pull the yarns too tight when changing colors.

Work the shaded stitches in contrast color.

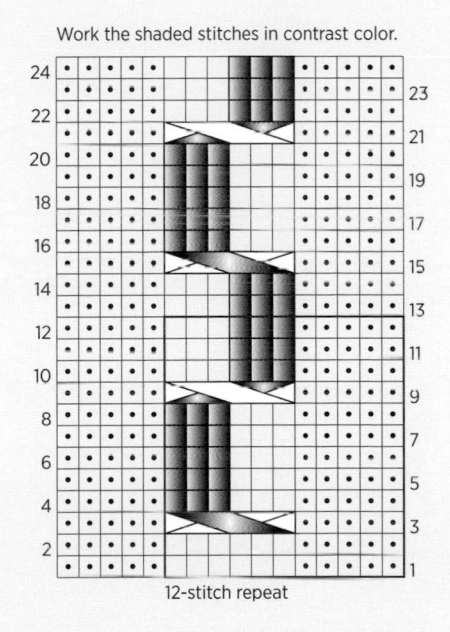

12-stitch repeat

Half-and-Half Colored Rope Cable

Rope Cable with Color Accent

Here's a 5/5L crossing cable that uses a second color for the third stitch of each half of the cable. The best way to work this is to cut long strands of the accent color and use one for each cable half; in other words, use the intarsia colorwork technique.

Work the center stitch of each half of the shaded crossings in contrast color.

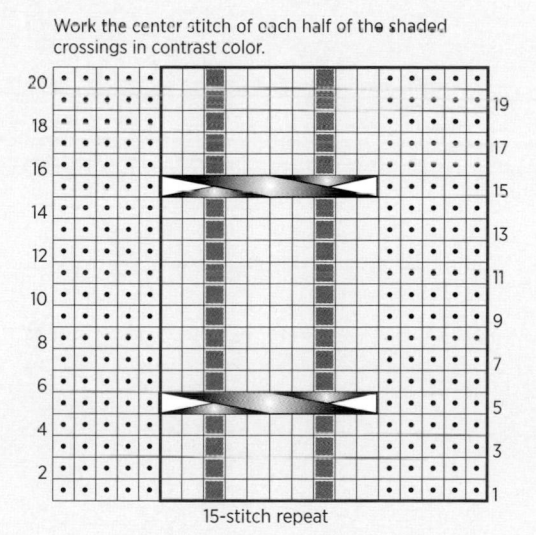

15-stitch repeat

Rope Cable with Color Accent

Half-and-Half Outward Cable with Color

This cable is worked like the half-and-half textured cable of the same name (page 166), but instead of using seed stitch on half the stitches, use a contrasting color. This is worked with the stranded colorwork technique.

Work the shaded stitches in contrast color.

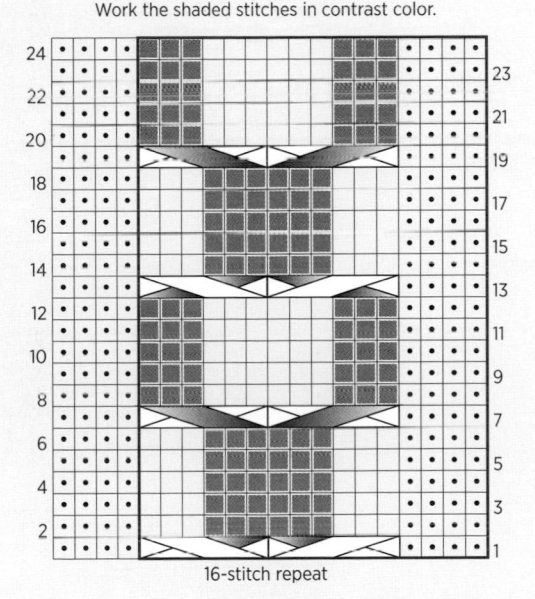

16-stitch repeat

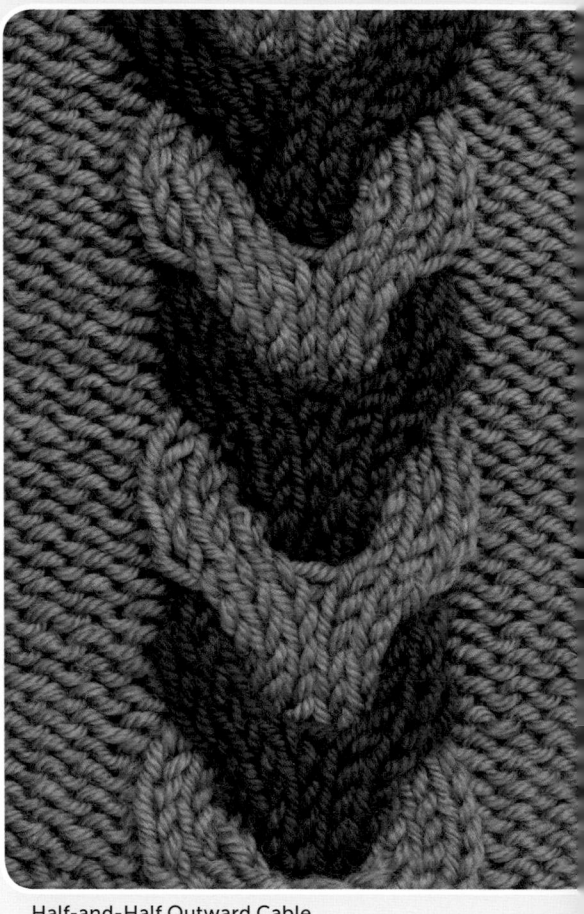

Half-and-Half Outward Cable
with Color

Colored Diamond with Bobble Clusters

Again, this is a repeat of a cable from the texture and bobble section (page 162). Use a contrasting color for bobble and cable stitches — all other stitches are worked in the main color. This design is best worked with the intarsia colorwork technique.

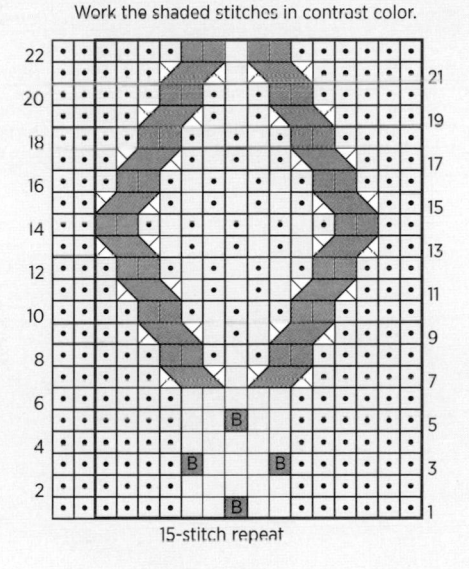

Work the shaded stitches in contrast color.

15-stitch repeat

Colored Diamond with Bobble Clusters

Allover Banded Cable in Two Colors

This is a great pattern for adding color. The result is a pattern of multitextured stripes that do a little dance every 16 rows. This is the same pattern as the Banded Cable in chapter 5, page 150.

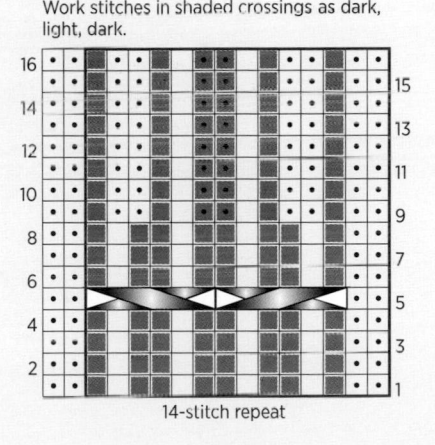

Work stitches in shaded crossings as dark, light, dark.

14-stitch repeat

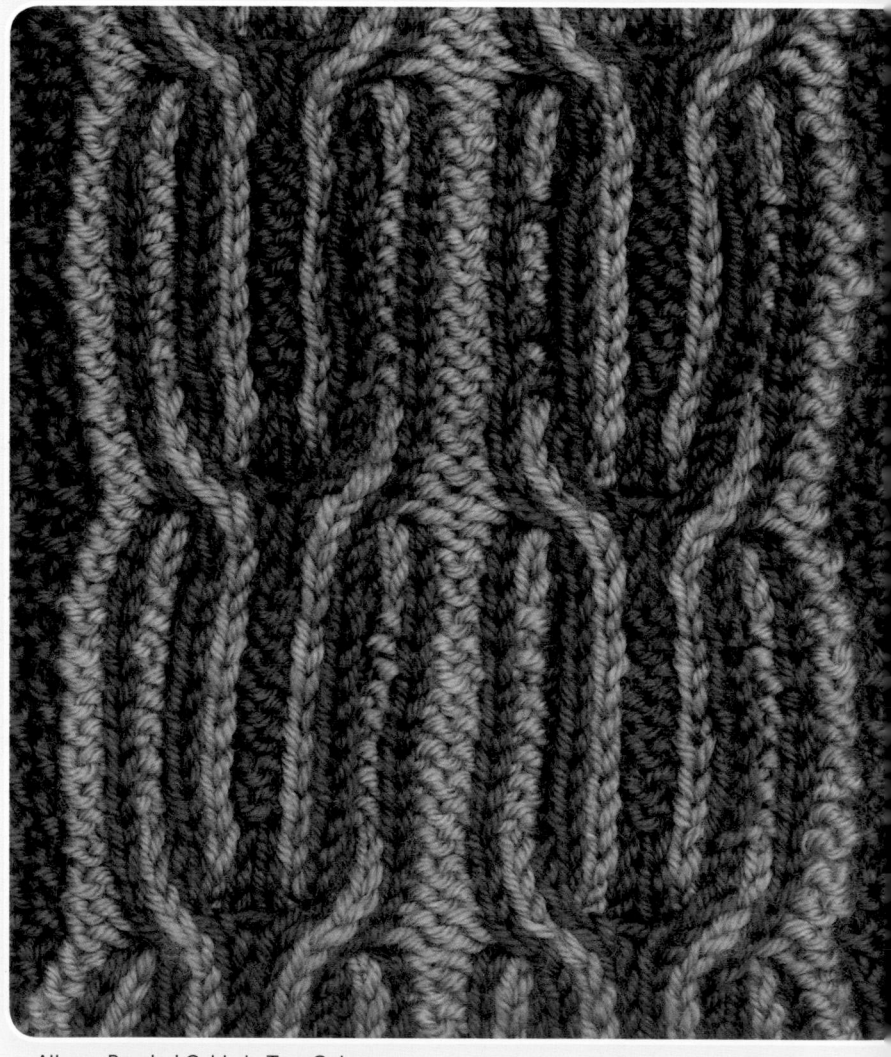

Allover Banded Cable in Two Colors

BEADING UP YOUR CABLES

Beads, wonderful shiny beads, can add a fantastical touch to your cables, whether for an elegant dress or just for fun. Here are four samples employing three different methods for adding beads to cables.

Rope Cable with Accent Beads

This cable is worked as for the Rope Cable with Color Accent on page 172, but instead of an accent color, use accent beads. To add a bead to the indicated stitch, which is the center stitch of each cable half, you'll use the hooked bead method shown here. Work the right-side rows of the 5/5 cable as follows. (Photo of beaded swatch and chart are on page 182.)

1 Work to the stitch to be beaded (the third and eighth of the cable).

2 Use crochet hook to pick up a bead.

3 Use crochet hook with bead to remove stitch from needle.

4 With tension on stich, hold stitch and hook in a straight line.

5 Slide bead down onto stitch.

6 Return stitch to left needle, and knit it.

Note: On Row 5 and all crossing rows, add a bead to the third stitch only.

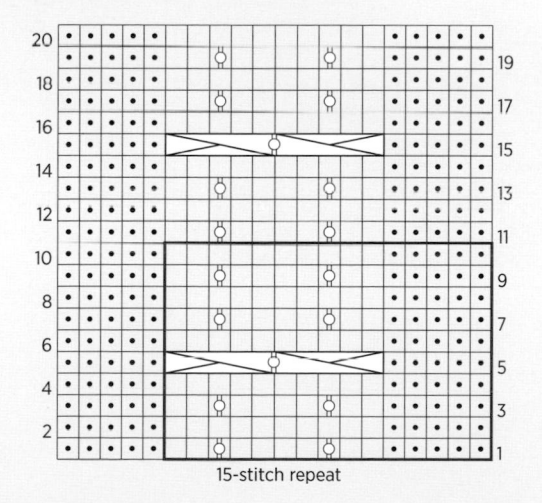

Rope Cable with Accent Beads

15-stitch repeat

Tips for Knitting with Beads

Here are some general guidelines for pairing yarn and beads and choosing a crochet hook if necessary.

YARN WEIGHT	SEED BEAD SIZE	HOOK SIZE (STEEL HOOK)
Lace-weight yarn	Size 11°	13/0.85 mm
Fingering-weight yarn	Size 8°	10/1.30 mm
DK and sport-weight yarn	Size 6°	5/1.9 mm

Prestringing Beads

For both the slipstitch bead method and for knitting and purling with beads (page 21), the beads must be strung onto the knitting yarn before you begin. Thread yarn onto a big eye beading needle or a dental floss threader, and then pick up the required number of beads, sliding them down the yarn toward the ball. When you need a bead, slide one up and work as directed.

Outward Cable with Beads

Outward Cable with Beads

Worked as for other outward cables presented in this book, this one uses an accent bead on the center of each half of the cable on every right-side row. The beads are added with the hooked-bead method as shown on page 180 for the Rope Cable with Accent Beads. On all but Row 1 of this pattern, add beads to the fifth and eighth stitch of the 12-stitch cable.

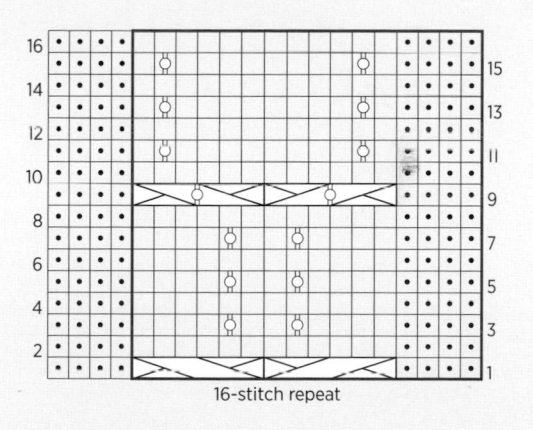

16-stitch repeat

Beads in the Honeycomb

This is a favorite pattern. It's great for mittens and hats because the beads are resting on top of slipped stitches — if it's cold outside, you'll never feel cold beads against your skin. For the slipstitch bead method, see page 21.

Beads in the Honeycomb

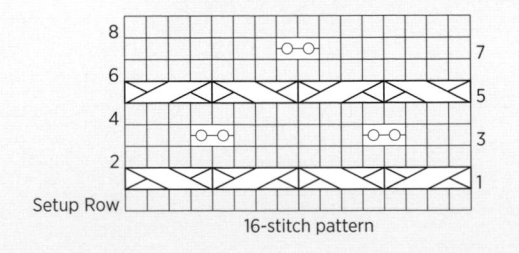

16-stitch pattern

Bead-It-All Diamond

Here is the Diamonds Large and Small motif (page 84) with beads worked into all the stitches of the cable crossings. See pages 188–189 for explanations of the beaded knit and beaded purl stitches. Be fore-warned that at the scale of this sample, things would become quite heavy if used for a long repeat. But with lace-weight yarn and tiny beads, the possibilities are endless.

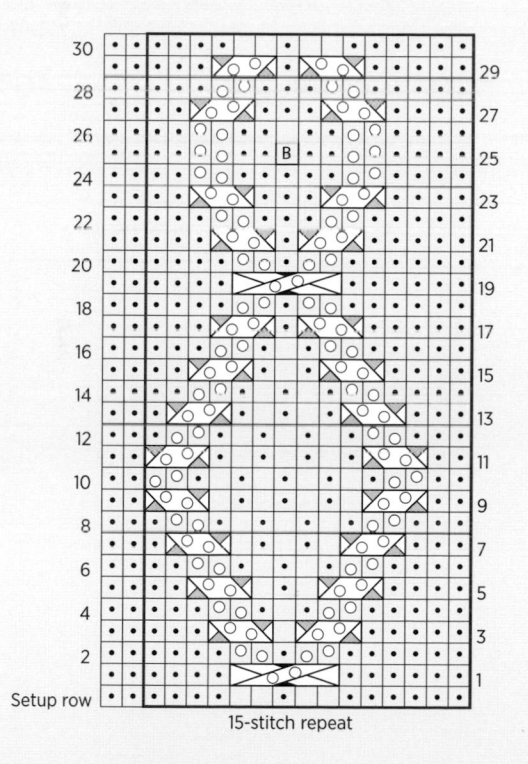

15-stitch repeat

Bead-It-All
Diamond

Beaded Knit Stitch

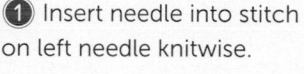

1 Insert needle into stitch on left needle knitwise.

2 Slide a bead up about ½" from needle.

3 Wrap the yarn around the needle, stopping the bead in the crux between the two needles.

4 Bring the bead through the stitch to the front to complete.

Beaded Purl Stitch

1 Insert needle into stitch on left needle purlwise.

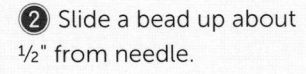

2 Slide a bead up about ½" from needle.

3 Wrap the yarn around the needle, stopping the bead in the crux between the two needles.

4 Push the bead through the stitch to the front side of the work to complete.

REVERSIBLE CABLE METHODS

Here are three ways to make cable patterns reversible. The first is to make cables on both the right and wrong sides of the work. The second is to make cables on one side and a simple rib pattern on the other. And the third method is to work a cable pattern with a knit and purl rib stitch. Now you can make cabled scarves that will look great no matter how they're worn.

Cables on Right and Wrong Sides

On the right side, 2/2L cables are turned every 4 rows, beginning with Row 3, and they are separated by 4 reverse stockinette stitches. On the wrong side, 2/2L cables are worked between the right-side cables every fourth row beginning with Row 4. The result is columns of cables separated by columns of textured reverse stockinette stitch on both sides.

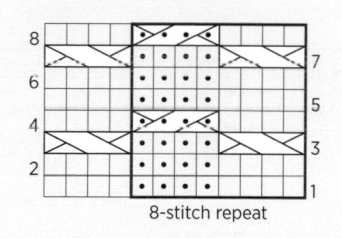

8-stitch repeat

Cables on
Right Side

Cables on
Wrong Side

Cables on Front, Ribs on Back

Working a knit cable that crosses over 2 stationary purl stitches maintains a rib pattern on the back of the fabric. The columns on the reverse side of the cables do pull in a little bit more than the others, but this just adds to the interest of the pattern.

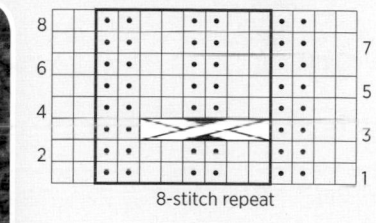

8-stitch repeat

Cables on Front, Right Side

Ribs on Back, Wrong Side

Knit 1, Purl 1 Cables

In this pattern 4/4R cables are worked in knit 1, purl 1 rib on a background of moss stitch. When it's time to turn the cable, simply maintain the rib pattern as established; that is, knit the knits and purl the purls. The ribbing pulls in so the purl stitches are hidden between the knit stitches on both sides.

Knit 1, Purl 1 Cables, Right Side

Work shaded stitches in k1, p1 ribbing.

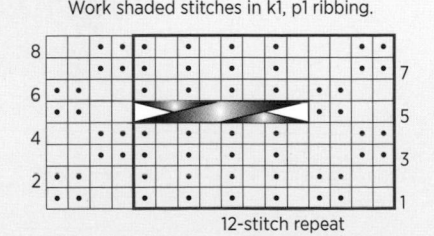

12-stitch repeat

Knit 1, Purl 1 Cables, Wrong Side

Knit 2, Purl 2 Cables

Here 4/4L and 4/4R cables are worked in knit 2, purl 2 ribbing. They are turned once every 8 rows and are staggered so that 4/4L cables are turned on Row 3 and 4/4R cables are between the left-crossing cables and turned on Row 7.

Knit 2, Purl 2 Cables, Wrong Side

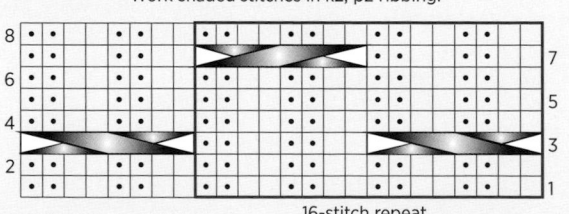

Knit 2, Purl 2 Cables, Right Side

Work shaded stitches in k2, p2 ribbing.

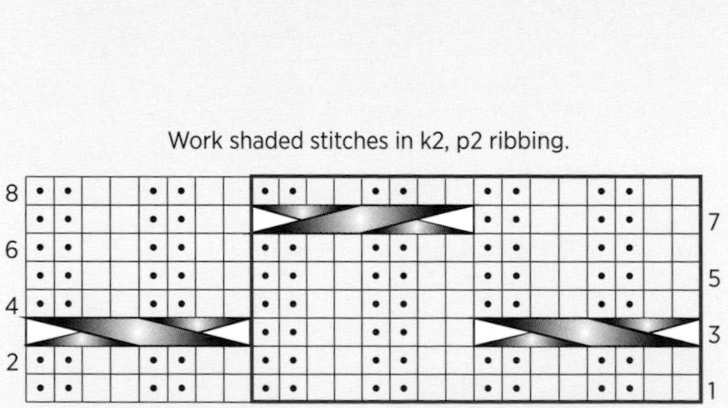

16-stitch repeat

CHAPTER 7

Design Considerations

Working highly textured patterns such as cables into your garments and other projects poses a few challenges that aren't present when knitting simpler patterns. Here are a few things to keep in mind when planning an original design.

BALANCING PATTERNS VERTICALLY

Ensure that smaller repeats divide evenly into the longest repeat.
If you want to use cable patterns together that have a different number
of rows in the repeat, it's easiest to combine cables that have repeats that
divide evenly into the longest cable repeat. For example, you could combine
a 32-row cable with a 16-row cable, an 8-row cable, a 4-row cable, and a
2-row cable; in the space of 32 rows, you can have one 32-row cable, two
16-row cables, four 8-row cables, eight 4-row cables and sixteen 2-row
cables. If you choose a 24-row cable as the longest, you can combine it with
a 12-row cable, an 8-row cable, a 6-row cable, a 4-row cable, and a 2-row
cable; in the space of 24 rows you can have one 24-row cable, two 12-row
cables, four 6-row cables, six 4-row cables, and twelve 2-row cables.

    Swatch to measure length of repeats. Always swatch your patterns
for gauge purposes. Check to see how many pattern repeats will fit into the
full length of your project. You may find that you can't begin and end with
a full pattern repeat but need, say, four and one-half repeats. If you want to
end with a full repeat, you'll have to begin with a half repeat. You could also
begin with a full repeat and end with a half. Another possibility would be to
begin and end with one-quarter of a repeat.

BALANCING PATTERNS HORIZONTALLY

Choose symmetry, if desired. If you have a wide central pattern flanked by other designs that include rope cables, you may opt to use right-crossing rope cables on one side of the center panel and left-crossing rope cables on the other side.

Here is a combination with an 18-row diamond pattern in the center, 2-stitch/2-row right and 2-stitch/2-row left twists, and 6-stitch/6-row right and 6-stitch/6-row left crossing cables. At the end of the swatch, Rows 1 and 2 are repeated for symmetry. (See chart on following page.)

Balanced Pattern

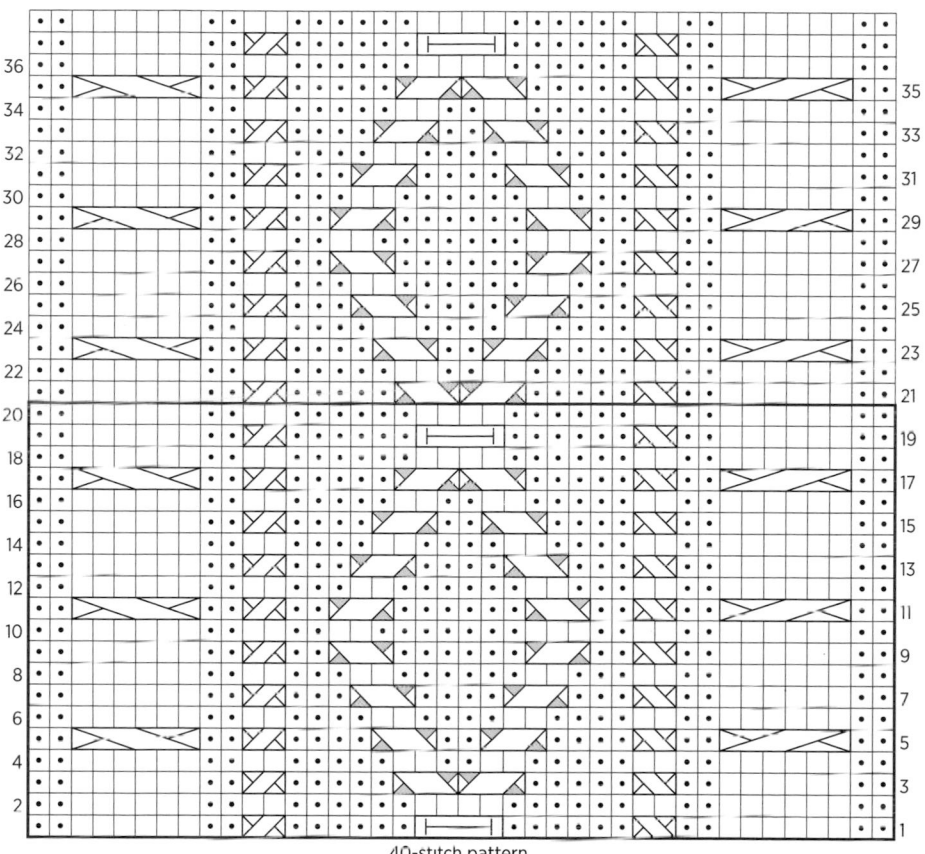

40-stitch pattern

Balanced Pattern Chart

Get the desired width. When you measure your individual cable swatches and calculate their combined width, you may find that you need more or fewer stitches to achieve the desired width of a garment. This is where those fillers come in handy. If you need more width, simply add a column or panel of one of the fillers described in chapter 5. If you were working the pattern presented on the previous page and needed just a tad more in the width, you could add an extra column of purl stitches on each side of one or all of the patterns. I wouldn't recommend using fewer than 2 purl stitches to separate patterns, so if you needed less width with this same pattern, you could eliminate the 6-stitch pattern at the beginning and end of the row and add another 2-stitch pattern, or you could change the 6-stitch rope cable to a 4-stitch rope cable. There are, of course, many possibilities.

COPING WITH TAKE-UP AND SPLAY

When turning cables, the action of crossing the stitches will make the fabric shrink in width. In other words, 6 stockinette stitches that measure 1 inch may measure only ¾ or ½ inch when worked as a 3/3 cable. So if you work a ribbing with the full complement of stitches and then begin to turn cables, the ribbing may have a slight ripple. This is called *cable take-up* and is visible in the swatch on page 206. At the bind-off end of a cabled piece, if you bind off the full complement of stitches, the piece will flare. This is called *cable splay* and is also visible in that same swatch.

Calculating Stitch Count

To compensate for the unevenness, you can increase for cables in the last row after the ribbing and decrease the cables before binding off. This example uses 3/3L cables with 2 purl stitches between the cables and at the edges. For the ribbing, cast on the number of stitches needed for the background and only 4 stitches for each 6-stitch cable. After the last row

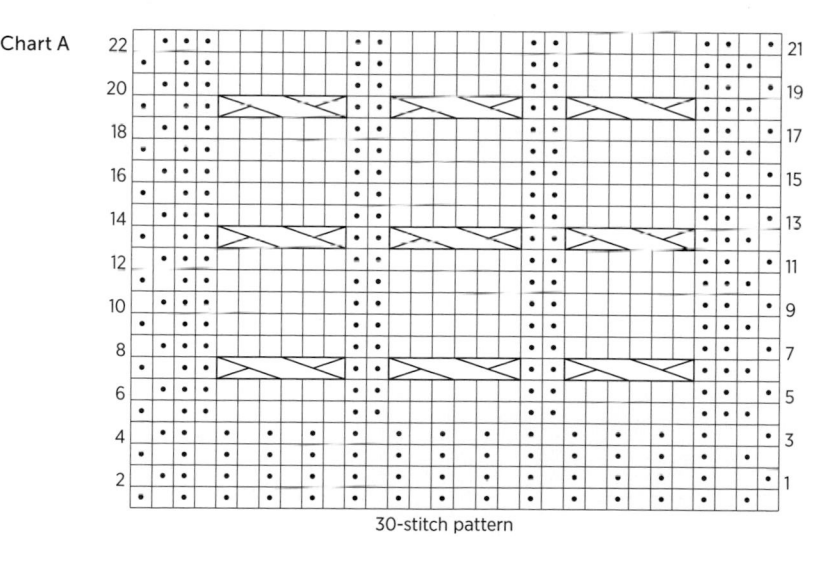

Chart A

30-stitch pattern

of ribbing, increase each set of 4 stitches designated for the cables to 6 stitches. It is important to increase at the places where the cables will be made, not just evenly across the row. When you are ready to bind off, say for a shoulder seam, you should decrease each 6-stitch cable back to 4 stitches. For the swatch below, the decreases were done on the turning round as follows: slip 3 stitches to cable needle and hold in front, k2tog, k1 from left needle, then ssk, k1 from cable needle.

The best way to figure out how many stitches to increase and decrease is to swatch and measure. First, make a swatch with the number of stitches needed for your cable pattern, and work the swatch with plain stockinette stitch. Then make a new swatch of the same number of stitches with turned cables. Measure the two widths to see how much take-up is in the cables. For the swatch on page 206, a 6-stitch cable is about the same width as 4 stockinette stitches, so for each 6-stitch cable you'd cast on 4 stitches for ribbing (or whatever you're starting with), then increase 2 stitches at each of the places where a cable will be worked.

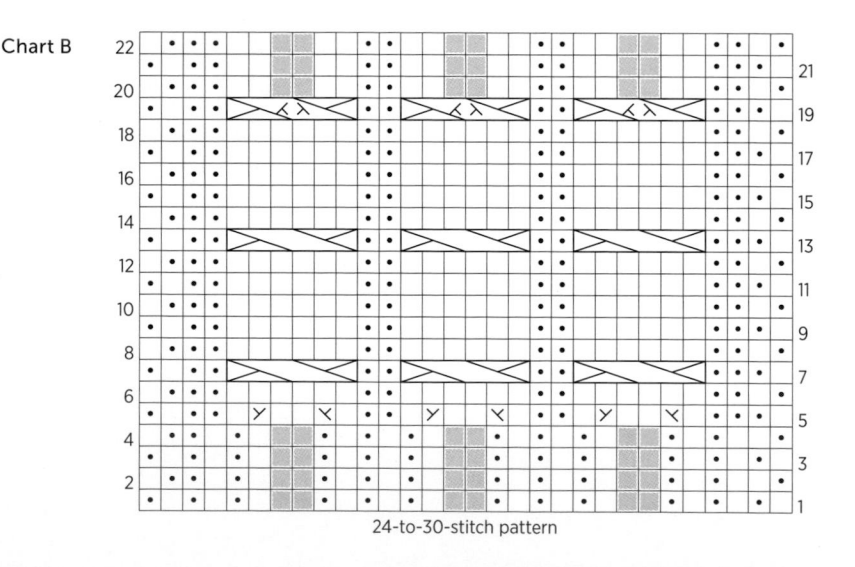

24-to-30-stitch pattern

cable splay

cable take-up

Knit from chart A, page 204,
without adjusting for take-up
and splay

Knit from chart B, page 205,
adjusted for take-up and
splay

DECREASING AND INCREASING IN CABLE PATTERNS

As mentioned in chapter 5, it's best to use a small filler pattern like seed, double seed, or moss stitch in places that need shaping, such as the underarms of bodies and sleeves. But there may be times when you want to increase or decrease a cable pattern. Here are a couple of scenarios.

Shaping for Rope Cables

Here is an example of a simple 3/3L cable pattern with 2 edge stitches on each side. The design requires that you decrease at the beginning and end of every sixth right-side row. If you simply stop turning cables when there are no longer 6 stitches available, you end up with a long column of narrowing stockinette stitch.

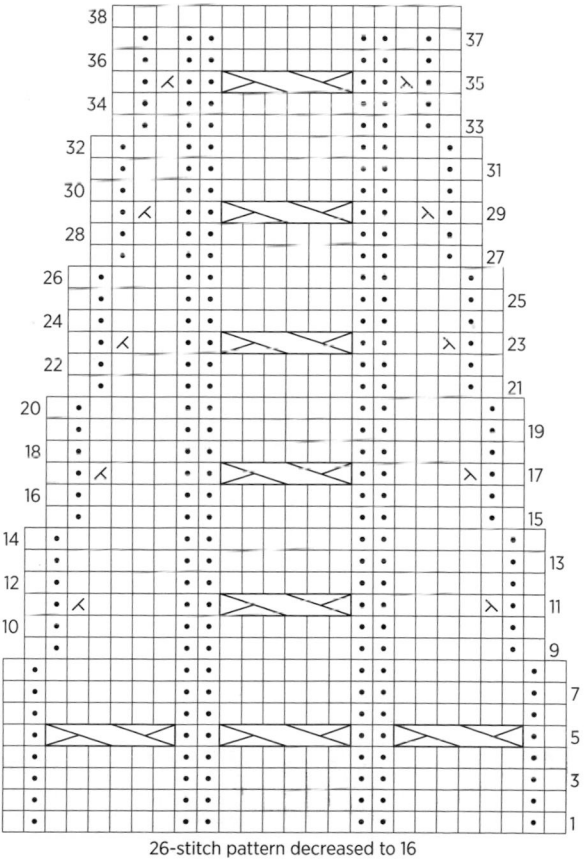

26-stitch pattern decreased to 16

Shaping Rope Cables

If you don't like the look of the previous swatch, you can simply turn the cables with fewer stitches. This swatch shows one full repeat; then 1 stitch is decreased from both the beginning and end of the turning rows. You want to maintain the 2 edge stitches, so the decreases are worked into the cables. The 3/3 cables become 3/2, then 2/2, 2/1, 1/1, and then they're gone! To increase, use this same system in reverse, for example, begin the first and last cables as 1/1, then increase to 2/1, 2/2, 3/2, and then 3/3 cables.

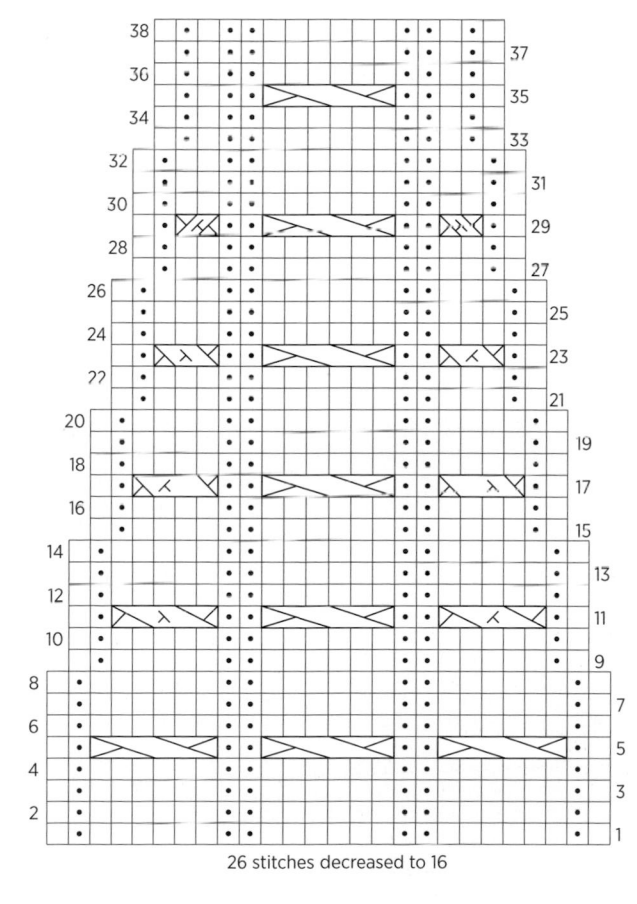

26 stitches decreased to 16

Shaping Rope Cables (alternate)

Decreasing an Allover Lattice

Here's an example of some finagling that you can do to keep a
lattice design in pattern while decreasing. It obviously becomes
increasingly difficult to decrease invisibly in more complex
patterns.

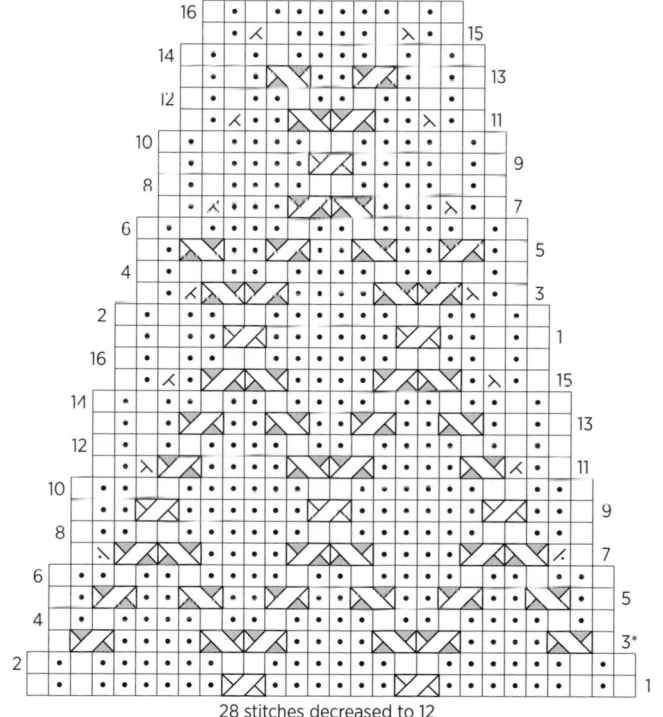

28 stitches decreased to 12

*First 4 stitches: K1, slip 1 purl to right needle, slip 1 knit onto cable needle
and hold in front, slip the purl back to the left needle and p2tog, k1 from cable
needle.

Last 4 stitches: Slip 1 purl to right needle, slip 1 knit onto cable needle and hold
in front, slip the purl back to the left needle, k1 from cable, p2tog, k1.

Allover Lattice Decreased

Index

bold = stitch chart

Allover Banded Cable in Two Colors, **170**, 178–79
allover patterns, 142–53

Balancing patterns, 200–203, **202**
Banded Cable Pattern, **150**, 150–51
Baroque Cable, 122–24, **124**
beading your cables
    Bead-It-All Diamond, **186**, 186–87
    beaded knit stitch, 188
    beaded purl stitch, 189
    Beads in the Honeycomb, 185, **185**
    Outward Cable with Beads, 184, **184**
    Rope Cable with Accent Beads, 180–82, **182**
    tips for knitting with beads, 183
binding cables, 167–69, **167–68**
bobbles
    Bobbles between Diamonds, 162, **162**
    Colored Diamond with Bobble Clusters, **176**, 176–77
    Half Diamond with Bobble Cluster, 163, **163**
    reverse stockinette stitch bobbles, 158–59
    seed stitch bobbles, 158–59
    stockinette stitch bobbles, 158
braids, 98–109
    3-Rib All-Knit Braid, 100, **100**
    3-Rib Knit and Purl Braid, 101, **101**
    4-Rib Knit and Purl Braid, 102, **102**
    6-Rib Braid, **108**, 108–9
    Braided Cables, **152**, 152–53
    combining braids with pretzels, 120–24
    Elongated 5-Rib Braid, **106**, 106–7
    Loose 5-Rib Braid, **104**, 104–5
    Tight 5-Rib Braid, 103, **103**

Cable crossings how-to
    1 over 1 left (1/1L), 32–33
    1 over 1 right (1/1R), 33–34
    1/2/1 left (1/2/1L), 31
    1/2/1 right (1/2/1R), 29–30

    2 over 2 left (2/2L), 34–35
    2 over 2 left (2/2L) alternate, 38
    2 over 2 right (2/2R), 36–37
    2 over 2 right (2/2R) alternate, 39
    3 over 1 left purl (3/1LP), 26–27
    3 over 1 right purl (3/1RP), 28
cables, simple, 44–63
    changing the proportion, 50–54
    combinations, 55–61
    defined, 12
    double-crossing cables, 62–63
    needle varieties, 22
    standard rope cables, 46–47
    tips for success, 40–41
    varying cable size, 48–49
charts
    calculating stitch count, **204–5**, 204–7
    counting rows, 42–43, **42–43**
    following a large chart, 125
Chunky Cables, 54, **54**
circles. *See* curves and circles
color, adding, 170–79
    Allover Banded Cable in Two Colors, **178**, 178–79
    Colored Diamond with Bobble Clusters, **176**, 176–77
    Half-and-Half Colored Rope Cable, **170**, 170–71
    Half-and-Half Outward Cable with Color, **174**, 174–75
    Rope Cable with Color Accent, **172**, 172–73
Condensed Cables, 52, **52**
counting rows, 42–43, **42–43**
curves and circles
    Disc Cables, 92, **92**
    Multidirectional Squiggles, 94, **94**
    Quatrefoil, 96–97, **97**
    Simple Curves, **90**, 90–91
    Squiggles, 93, **93**
    Stand-Alone or Closed Ring Circle, 95, **95**

Decreasing in cable patterns, **208**, 208–13, **210**, **212**
Diagonal Grid, 75, **75**
diamonds
    Bead-It-All Diamond, **186**, 186–87
    Bobbles between Diamonds, 162, **162**
    Colored Diamond with Bobble Clusters, **176**, 176–77
    Diamond with Rope Cables, **86**, 86–87
    Diamonds Large and Small, **84**, 84–85
    Dressed Diamonds Large and Small: Even Number of Stitches, **160**, 160–61
    Dressed Diamonds Large and Small: Odd Number of Stitches, **156**, 156–57
    Half Diamond with Bobble Cluster, 163, **163**
    No-Cross Diamond, **82**, 82–83
    Right-Crossing Diamond, **78**, 78–79
    Simple Symmetrical Diamond, **76**, 76–77
    Staggered Diamonds, **146**, 146–47
    Staggered Diamonds Variation, **148**, 148–49
    Stand-Alone or Closed Ring, **88**, 88–89
    Wrapped-Crossing Diamond, 80–81, **81**
Disc Cables, 92, **92**
Double Cables
    Half-and-Half Outward, **166**, 166–67
    Separated Inward, 56, **56**
    Separated Outward, 55, **55**
    United Inward, 58, **58**
    United Outward, 57, **57**
double seed stitch, 130, **130**
double-crossed cable ribbing, 138, **138**
Double-Crossing Cables
    4-Stitch, 62, **62**
    7-Stitch, 63, **63**
double-crossing cables, how to work
Double-Knot Cable, **120**, 120–21

Elongated 5-Rib Braid, **106**, 106–7
Elongated Cables, 50, **50**
    Super-Elongated Cables, 51, **51**

Floating zigzag ribbing, 139, **139**

Honeycomb stitch, 131, **131**
    Beads in the Honeycomb, 185, **185**
    mini-honeycomb, 132, **132**
Hourglass Cable, 60–61, **61**
hourglass ribbing, 141, **141**

Increasing in cable patterns, **208**, 208–11, **210**

Knit-over-purl cable crossings
    3 over 1 left purl (3/1LP), 26–27
    3 over 1 right purl (3/1RP), 28
knitting cables without a cable needle
    1 over 1 left (1/1L), 32–33
    1 over 1 right (1/1R), 33–34
    2 over 2 left (2/2L), 34–35
    2 over 2 left (2/2L) alternate, 38
    2 over 2 right (2/2R), 36–37
    2 over 2 right (2/2R) alternate, 39

Larger and Even Smaller Cables, 49, **49**
lattice stitch
    decreasing an allover lattice, **212**, 213
    tight lattice stitch, 134, **134**
    woven-basket lattice stitch, 135, **135**
Lattice with Right and Left Crossings, **144**, 144–45
Lattice with Right Crossings, **142**, 142–43
Left-Crossing Cable (3/3L), 46, **46**
left-crossing cables, how to work, 23–24

Mini-cable ribbing, 136, **136**
mini-honeycomb stitch, 132, **132**
moss stitch, 129, **129**
Multidirectional Squiggles, 94, **94**

Needle varieties, 22

Pretzels, 98, 110–20
    4-Rib Asymmetrical Pretzel, **112**, 112–13
    4-Rib Symmetrical Pretzel, **110**, 110–11
    5-Rib Pretzel, **114**, 114–15
    6-Rib Pretzel, **116**, 116–17
    8-Rib Pretzel, **118**, 118–19
    combining pretzels with braids, 120–24

Quatrefoil, 96–97, **97**

Reversible cable methods
    Cables on Front, Ribs on Back, **192**, 192–93
    Cables on Right and Wrong Sides, **190**, 190–91
    Knit 1, Purl 1 Cables, **194**, 194–95
    Knit 2, Purl 2 Cables, **196**, 196–97
ribbing
    double-crossed cable ribbing, 138, **138**
    floating zigzag ribbing, 139, **139**
    hourglass ribbing, 141, **141**
    mini-cable ribbing, 136, **136**
    ribbing plus cable, 137, **137**
    squiggles and twists, 140, **140**
Right-Crossing Cable (3/3R), 47, **47**
right-crossing cable, how to work, 25–26
rope cables
    Binding Rope Cables, 167, **167**
    Half-and-Half Colored, **170**, 170–71
    Half-and-Half Textured, **164**, 164–65
    Rope Cable with Accent Beads, 180–82, **182**
    Rope Cable with Color Accent, **172**, 172–73
    shaping for rope cables, **208**, 208–211, **210**

Seed stitch, 128, **128**
    double seed stitch, 130, **130**
Simple Curves, **90**, 90–91

Simple Zigzag, **66**, 66–67
Smaller Cables, 48, **48**
Snaking Cable, 59, **59**
splay. *See* take-up and splay
Squiggles, 93, **93**
    Multidirectional Squiggles, 94, **94**
squiggles and twists, 140, **140**
Stand-Alone or Closed Ring Circle, 95, **95**
Stand-Alone or Closed Ring Diamond, **88**, 88–89
symbols defined, 14–21

Take-up and splay, **204–5**, 204–7
terminology, 12–13
tips for cable success, 40–41
trinity stitch, 133, **133**

Varying the Crossings, 53, **53**

Woven-basket lattice stitch, 135, **135**

X-crossings
    1-Stitch X, 71, **71**
    2-Stitch X, 70, **70**
    3-Stitch X, **68**, 68–69
    Acute X, 74, **74**
    Enlarged X, **72**, 72–73

Zigzag
    floating zigzag ribbing, 139, **139**
    Simple Zigzag, **66**, 66–67

Acknowledgments

Thanks once again to the wonderful staff at Storey Publishing for seeing me through yet another book. Thanks especially to my editor, Gwen Steege, whose enthusiasm is seemingly boundless, and to Deborah Balmuth for her continued support. Thanks to Mary Velgos for another beautiful book design, and to Mars Vilaubi for the crisp and clear photography; thanks to Melinda Slaving and Corey Cusson for tending to schedules and other details.

Thanks also to Kate Atherly for her careful technical edit and many helpful suggestions, and thanks once again to Debby and Lynda Gemmell of Cabin Fever for help with their Shelridge Farm Soft Touch DK, which was used for all the samples.

And, as always, thank you, Philippe, for your love and encouragement.